PRAISE FOR
When We Were Colored

"Reading *When We Were Colored* was like conversation and tea with a wise neighbor till I considered just how strong a woman would have to be, and what it would a cost a mother, to so passionately desire her children to grow up to 'soar, across the land and the nation, above classes and creeds and color of skin,' yet always to remain practical, upbeat, and resourceful in the face of chronic prejudice. I suspect that Eva Rutland's heroic endeavors have been repeated over the years in many homes, but rarely has the story been told so well."

Sarah B. Hrdy, Professor Emerita, University of
California, Davis, and author of *Mother Nature*

"*When We Were Colored* has an amusing 'Mama Knows Best' sensibility. The book also gives the reader a serious look at the West's black middle class—usually invisible in American storytelling."

Janet Clayton, Assistant Managing Editor,
Los Angeles Times

"Eva Rutland's evocation of race, place, and time has near perfect poignancy and verisimilitude. With a wonderful blend of intimacy and sociology, *When We Were Colored* recaptures the wisdom, resiliency, and love of a family overcoming a world once oppressively divided into black and white."

David Levering Lewis, Professor of History,
New York University, and recipient of the
Pulitzer Prize for B̶i̶o̶g̶r̶a̶p̶h̶y̶

"Eva Rutland . . . shares many truths about being a 'Negro Mother.' With pride in her heritage and a forgiving heart toward the abuses of the era, this Southern woman describes her journey from Atlanta to Tuskegee to Sacramento. She roots her family firmly and deftly in the black middle class in California, preparing her children to succeed. How she does it is a charming tale told by an authentic storyteller offering an abundance of compassion, insight, and humor. Enjoy!"

Maria Henson, winner of the 1992 Pulitzer Prize for Editorial Writing

"Eva Rutland's memoir vividly conveys the warmth, wit, humor, and homespun wisdom that helped her guide her children through the challenges of thriving in a segregated society on the cusp of transformative change. The story . . . is as well-written as it is engaging . . . It is inspiring and instructive for any mother interested in raising children who are healthy and whole."

Shelley Fisher Fishkin, Professor of English and Director of American Studies, Stanford University

"Eva Rutland tells the kinds of stories that form the foundation of civilization—emotionally rich, immensely satisfying tales of family, friendship, and basic humanity. Her narrative gift lets us share a perspective we'd never know on our own— yet also discover how universal her experience has been. . . . This is profound storytelling wearing a deceptively simple wrap: clean, transparent prose that introduces readers to a world they will very much enjoy."

Howard Weaver, two-time Pulitzer Prize–winning reporter and editor

WHEN WE WERE
Colored

A *mother's story*

Eva Rutland

Ena R.

IWP, Book Publishers
Sacramento, California

IWP, Book Publishers
1201 K Street, Suite 970
Sacramento, CA 95814
Tel: (916) 456-7080   www.iwpbookpublishers.com

Rutland's story of the incident of Elsie and God, as found in chapter 2 of *When We Were Colored* by Eva Elsie Rutland, first appeared in *Redbook* magazine in the '50s. Reprinted courtesy of *Redbook.*

The story of the morning the swings were empty, as found in chapter 2 of *When We Were Colored* by Eva Elsie Rutland, is reprinted by permission of *Woman's Day* magazine, part of Hachette Filipacchi Media.

"Taught to Hate" by Eva Rutland, copyright June 1952, is excerpted with the permission of *Ladies' Home Journal,* Meredith Corporation.

The poetry on page 129 is from *The Prophet* by Kahlil Gibran, copyright 1923 by Kahlil Gibran and renewed 1951 by Administrators C.T.A. of Kahlil Gibran Estate and Mary G. Gibran. Used by permission of Alfred A. Knopf, a division of Random House, Inc.

Ordering Information
Quantity sales. Special discounts are available on quantity purchases by corporations, associations, and others. For details, contact the "Special Sales Department" at the IWP, Book Publishers address above.

Orders for college textbook/course adoption use. Please contact IWP, Book Publishers at (916) 456-7080.

Orders by U.S. trade bookstores and wholesalers. Please contact Biblio Distribution, 4501 Forbes Blvd. #200, Lanham, MD 20706. Tel: (800) 462-6420, www.bibliodistribution.com.

Printed in the United States of America

Cataloging-in-Publication Data
Rutland, Eva.
When we were colored : a mother's story / Eva Rutland.
     p. cm.
     Revised edition.
     ISBN–10: 1-934-178-00-4 ISBN–13: 978-1-934178-00-3
1. Rutland, Eva—Biography. 2. African Americans—Biography. 3. African Americans—Civil rights. 4. African Americans—Georgia—Atlanta—Biography. 5. Atlanta (Ga.)—Biography. 6. Mothers—United States—Biography.
7. California—Biography. I. Title.
E185.97.R94 W46 2007
323.092—dc22   2006937985

FIRST EDITION
12 11 10 09 08 07   10 9 8 7 6 5 4 3 2

Contents

To Bill

and the children—

Elsie, Billy, Pat,

and especially Ginger,

who says,

"It's a good thing you had us—

else you wouldna' had a book."

Introduction

When We Were Colored was first published in 1964 under the title *The Trouble with Being a Mama*. Back then, as a "colored" mother, I was seeking common ground with white mothers, a way to let all mothers know that we had so much in common. My black children were just like their white children, filled with all the talent, hope, beauty, and insecurities of childhood, just as precious and just as fragile. Before integration, before affirmative action—when segregation was the norm, discrimination was legally tolerated, and blacks were second-class citizens—it was, I thought, an important story to tell.

Now, almost fifty years later, life in America has changed, but my story is as relevant today as it was then. It transcends the black-white divide. It's really about the challenges and fears that all mothers face as we struggle to raise healthy, happy, productive children. The era in which I raised my children is long gone, but the troubles I encountered afflict today's mamas too.

My biggest trouble with being a mama, especially a black mama, was my unfamiliarity with the rapidly changing world into which my children were born. I was born in Atlanta, Georgia, during the olden days when grass was on the lawn, pot was a cooking utensil, webs were for spiders, and civil rights were for white folks. We lived in the house my grandfather, a former slave, built soon after the Civil War. The neighborhood was still full of big houses when I was born, probably originally occupied by well-to-do Jews, for the Jewish synagogue was only two blocks from our house. During the big depression years of my teens, most of the well-to-do had moved away and three or more poor white families crowded into the big old houses previously occupied by one family. Besides us, three stable black families lived on our block, one on either side of us and one across the street. A few poor blacks huddled in tiny shacks in two back alleys nearby.

Since we had a telephone and the biggest yard, I classed myself with my well-off friends who lived in the colored sections of town. I guess I would have been a bit of a snob had it not been for my mother, who spread the welcome mat for one and all. Noticing the variety of people who were welcomed at our house, Owen, my cousin, once asked her, "Aunt Eva, do you know everybody in town?"

"If they're worth knowing," she answered.

To Mama, however, it seemed everyone was worth knowing, from Mrs. Brookman, the very proper German lady with whom Mama shared kitchen goodies and fresh fruit, to drunken Miss Flora, who reeled in each Monday to help with the wash. We played with the poor blacks from the back alleys and the poor white children too. Not one kid, black or white, was banned from our yard, which became the neighborhood playground.

I didn't like where we lived. I wanted to live in one of the segregated, totally all-black communities where I went to school, played, and attended parties with my close black friends. I had to trudge with my brother Ed through several all-white neighborhoods to reach our private elementary school on black Atlanta University's campus on the west side. We had to board two streetcars to reach the Fourth Ward, on the edge of downtown where many families of Atlanta's black elite lived. My Aunt Mamie lived there, on Auburn Avenue. I often stayed with her, roaming her two story house with central heat, reading for hours at the colored Carnegie Library only one block away, or traveling three blocks to watch my pharmacist father make medicine on the third floor of the Odd Fellows Building in Atlanta's bustling black business district.

As I look back, I realize that I lived in two worlds, one almost totally white and the other almost totally black—but not quite. For no matter where I was, policemen, streetcar conductors, and grocery clerks were white. Actually, I was happy in both worlds and could easily switch from one to the other. When my children were born, the two worlds had begun to mix and herein lies my story. I wrote *The Trouble with Being a Mama* almost fifty years ago. When my daughter read excerpts of it at my husband's funeral last year, so many people asked me where they could get a copy, I realized it still has relevance today.

As you read this book, I hope you will forgive my husband's outrageous cussing and his careless use of the "n" word. For him it was often a term of endearment. After all, his best buddy was his "main"—well, you know what.

Forgive me too. I'm not quite up on today's politically correct phrasing. We were colored in my day or Negro, definitely not African American, a term, by the way, I dislike. With the exception of Indians—excuse me, Native Americans—my black ancestors reached these shores long before most other people who call themselves just plain Americans arrived.

Also, I'm apt to call a crazy person "crazy" or even hint that "he's not dealing with a full deck." I might even call a blind person "blind," even when people in the know tell me I'm supposed to say "visually impaired."

Oh, and another thing—my children tell me my views of Malcolm X are outdated. By the time he was gunned down he was no longer preaching hate. So, my apologies to Mr. X.

Anyway, this book was written during the 1950s and '60s "when we were colored," and I told it like it was. So I warn you, try not to be offended—just enjoy.

Eva Rutland at age 12 in Atlanta, Georgia

1
The Trouble Is...

The trouble with being a mama is you worry too much. You worry about why Tommy spits up his milk and smells so sour, why Archie sucks his thumb, why Annie can't grasp Spanish, why that "absolute doll" won't ask Doris to the platter-hop, why Patty has so many boyfriends, how on earth to keep eight wriggling Cub Scouts still enough to make eight sparkling pairs of earrings for eight sparkling mamas' sparkling Christmas presents (well, seven—you're willing to forgo yours), how to get children who don't like eggs to eat good solid breakfasts, how to stretch the budget to include those nourishing eggs they leave on their plates, how to calm a husband who doesn't like eggs left on plates that a budget had to be stretched to include, why other kids look so scrubbed and yours look so grimy, what to do about smelly feet (why doesn't somebody invent sneakers that don't make feet sweat?), how to get a bass fiddle and four-foot boy to school together without carrying them yourself, how to discipline Billy without warping his personality, how to keep your husband from warping Billy's person, how to iron blouses with no cat faces, how to get Tommy to wear his pants around his waist instead of his hips, how to straighten curly hair, how to curl straight hair, and how to make uniforms for Girl Scouts who are going to serve in the children's hospital (you know this is good training but you never could look a needle straight in the eye—and why don't the uniforms come ready-made?). And if you're a Negro mother you have a few extra worries. Will Sarah be accepted at Mr. Diddlywhat's Dancing School and can the kids swim in the public swimming pool? How adequate is Joey's segregated school or how integrated is his integrated school? And what to do when somebody calls him a "nigger"?

My big trouble is I wasn't trained to be a mama—well, not the worrying type anyway. My mama never worried. Oh, about fundamentals, like how to pay the bills and what to cook for dinner. But about children, no. You bathed 'em, you fed 'em, and you made 'em behave—and that was it. My mama was a schoolteacher but I don't believe she ever read a psychology book in her life. She had one method of discipline—a peachtree switch applied vigorously around one's legs. Her approach was to get rid of a bad habit—and who ever heard of personality? I remember my aunt couldn't stop one of my cousins from sucking her thumb so she sent her over to my mama. Mama broke the habit in three days. She simply tied said thumb to the bedpost out of reach of said mouth, with no thought of substitutions and no qualms about said child's emotional stability and security and whether said child's parents quarreled in the presence of said child. Said child now has married, has thumb-sucking children of her own, and from what I can see has a well-rounded personality, suffering no ill effects or frustrations from said thumb incident.

The only time my mother used psychology (and it was strictly the homemade or mother-wit kind—I'm sure she never got this out of any book) was when one of her own cherubs snitched three pennies out of her purse to purchase an oversized cherry lollipop. This was in the days when allowances were unheard of and any store-bought delicacy had to be strictly accounted for. The source of the lollipop was immediately traced and punishment promptly administered. Not the peachtree switch variety. Stealing was a major infraction and called for major surgery. The punishment (get this, now) was for the culprit to wear a blindfold for three hours and pretend he was blind. I really thought he was and set up such a howl that he had to peek under the blindfold to show me that he could really see. I never did see the connection between the blindfold and stealing, but the punishment had its effect and served as an example to Mama's other children as well as the culprit. It scared the daylights out of me, and I don't remember another incident of stealing in the history of our entire family.

Nowadays the punishment for stealing is not so simple. One must first see that the child is loved, has some valuable possessions of his own, is made a junior partner in the family firm, is presented with an itemized tabulation of how Dad's income is spent, and is provided with some small service that will enable him to earn the money to buy whatever his little heart desires. Then, as I think I read somewhere, "Johnny no longer has to try to satisfy his deepest hunger—his hunger for love—by making forays on his mother's purse."

But, as I said, Mama was not confused by psychology. And for the "nigger" problem, she had one answer—you were not a "nigger," you were a *Negro*, a word uttered with such dignity that you were proud of the fact and sorry for the ignorant so-and-so who didn't know the difference. As a matter of fact, Mama was not only conscious of her own dignity and worth.

She was absolutely and irrevocably conscious of everyone else's dignity and worth, and that took some doing in the neighborhood in which we lived—a strange mixture of races and classes and creeds. The Jews centered around their synagogue on Pryor Street, the middle-class white people on Formwalt, the poorer whites across the street, and the poorer Negroes huddled in the shacks on the alley in back of our lot.

The neighborhood was not new to Mama. She had been born there when there was nothing but trees around and a creek, long since dried up. Her father had built our house long before the Jewish families built all around them. Mama used to slip out to wash diapers and help in their kitchens and slip back in before Grandpa got home. Grandpa was proud, and his shoe shop on Whitehall Street had thrived. He brought sugar and flour in by the barrelfuls, and he kept his children—all eleven of them—warmly clothed, and he didn't mean to see them in "anybody's kitchen." He saw them all finish college before he died. Mama had been there during the riot between the Negroes and whites. She often told how Mrs. McBride, their white neighbor on the hill, had come down during Atlanta's 1906 race riots and said to her mother, "Well, Emma, if the white folks come, you all come up to our house, and if the black folks come, we'll come down here. That way, we'll all be safe." Good neighbors, that's the way Mama felt, and she kept feeling that way, even as the neighborhood grew more complex.

And Mama's love and compassion for everyone had its effect on me. I'd retire shivering behind a chair when Miss Flora from up in the alley came reeling and rocking in to use "Miz' Eva's" telephone. She could use it if she didn't want to call the police.

And then there was the witch that lived around the corner from us. I know she was a witch because all the children said so and she looked like one. I can see her now, bent and wizened, wispy white hair straggly under the black shawl, sweeping her walk with a long straw broom and followed by a slinky black cat. Her big yard was encircled with a heavy iron fence wired with electricity, or so went the rumor. To even touch it meant instant death, to say nothing of climbing it to reach the luscious green apples that hung temptingly from a limb above or the purple grapes whose vines entwined it. The gate had a heavy latch, controlled, it was said, by a special switch inside the house—one glance in a special mirror identified you as friend or foe and you were in or out, whichever the old witch preferred. I definitely preferred out and always walked cautiously on the other side of the street. But Mama insisted she was no witch, just poor old Mrs. Brookman who was lonely and unhappy because Mr. Brookman had killed himself when Germany lost the First World War, and "run over and take the poor old soul a pan of these hot rolls."

As I said, Mama had no use for psychology or witches or black magic or childish fears.

So down the street and around the corner I went, careful not to touch the iron fence, lifting the latch with one finger, wishing it wouldn't budge, down the long walk, past the slinky black cat, into the darkened house, carefully shutting the door behind me—just me and the witch and a pan of hot rolls.

"Ach!" exclaimed the witch. "How mein fraulëin has grown." And taking the rolls, still gibbering in an unknown tongue, she led me toward the back of the house. Mama will be sorry, I thought.

But she only wanted to give me a bucket of the luscious apples and I escaped happily, careful to touch only the latch and thankful that the witch bore me no ill will.

Of course Mama's idiosyncrasies also had their advantages. Miss Nancy, the black lady who lived next door, warned Mama not to let us play with those "alley brats," the poor blacks from the back alleys. She was careful not to suggest banning the poor white children. Perhaps because Miss Nancy, like my grandfather, was a former slave and still retained a cautious respect for all white people. Mama paid no attention to Miss Nancy. We could play with anybody, white or black, and anybody could borrow anything. This was during the Depression years when everybody was poor.

We were poor too. At least I guess we were poor. My father was a pharmacist and during most of my childhood worked in a prescription shop. In those days few of the medicines came bottled or capsuled as they seem to come now, and I used to love to watch my daddy as he mixed several powders on a marble slab—mixing, mixing, then smoothing and cutting into exact portions and expertly pressing each portion into a tiny capsule. It was an artistic operation that never failed to fascinate me. I used to like to wander among the strange-smelling boxes and bottles on the shelves in back of the shop. One bottle I especially remember—second bottle from the end, third shelf down. It was called "creosotonic." Daddy used to give it to us for colds, and I loved the taste.

Things were not always easy for Daddy, especially during the Depression. At various times he worked as a bellhop or waiter in hotels, and for a long time as a waiter in railroad dining cars. Even in the roughest times he never allowed me to look for work downtown for "you know how these white men are about Negro girls." Nor did he allow the boys to bellhop or work in any of the hotels because "in such a situation a Negro boy can get in trouble through no fault of his own."

Anyway, we were so much better off than many of our Negro neighbors that I think the help Mama had—Mr. Anthony or Miss Flora or Miss Bessie who came to wash (not always, as I can distinctly remember helping with the wash myself, with three tin tubs and an iron pot in which to boil clothes) or Lynn or Chester or any of the succession of teenage boys from the alley who came to bring in wood or coal or scrub the kitchen floor or dust—were hired for a number of reasons. Partly they were hired because Mama really believed in gracious living. Whether this was because of a deep feeling that a lady did not do hard work or because she was fundamentally lazy or because she was really more interested in a lively bridge game or a chat with a neighbor than she was in a spotless house, I do not know. I do know that housework was not for her. She worked the living daylights out of me, and even now I can see her rocking on the porch, her eye on the living room where Lynn was dusting—"Lynn, honey, you missed that chair over there." Part of it was not that Mama actually needed help or could afford it but because she really wanted to help those who had less than herself; and she had a way of helping that left a man his pride and self-respect. What Mama had meant to these people became ever so clear to me when I went home for her funeral and observed the many, many people who came to pay their respects—Lynn from the back alley, married now, with children and a better home; drunken Miss Flora; Mr. W., the white man who had lived for a few years across the street; the white grocer two blocks away, as well as Atlanta's Negro society from the plush homes across town. All of them had loved and been loved by "Miss Eva."

So if we were poor, we had compensations—a telephone, a big yard, and Mr. Anthony. Mr. Anthony lived only a few

blocks away and seemed to exist entirely on the vegetables he
shared from Miss Eva's garden and the few dollars "Dr. Neal"
(my daddy) gave him. He loved gardening, and after a cup of
black coffee and a good conversation (or I should say mono-
logue) in which he explained in exquisite detail the various
books of the Bible, he could work all day outside with a rake,
a hoe, and a definite green thumb. Our yard flourished with
roses, corn, and collard greens.

Of course the gardener's green thumb must have been
considerably helped by his predecessor, the cow. The cow belonged to a Jewish lady, Mrs. Goldstein, who had heard of
Mama's lend-lease policy and requested the upper lot for
grazing purposes in exchange for a share of the milk. So the
cow did her part toward fertilizing the land. That nobody ever
complained but us kids is proof of how the neighborhood had
deteriorated since Grandpa's day. And although I could never
understand Mama's position (a cow in the yard was too
much!), after four kids and a running battle with the local
dairyman (my kids each drink at least a quart a day), I have at
last come to understand Mrs. Goldstein's position. She had a
brood that followed her around when she came to fetch the
cow for milking. But Sophia is the only one I remember—and
that only because of the candy.

I had a brother, Ed, who dearly loved to cook—not funda-
mental things like collards and cornbread but candy and cookies, all sorts of dainties. And that was another peculiarity of
Mama's—he made it, we ate it, and I had to clean up. But that's
beside the point. On this particular day he emerged from the
kitchen and approached us at hopscotch.

"Want some candy?" I glanced at the creamy white tid-
bits, wondering how many pans were awaiting me. Sophia
had another problem. Poised on one foot in the middle of the

hopscotch square, she eyed the candy and said plaintively, "I can't eat it if it has lard in it."

My brother's eyes sparkled.

"Oh, it doesn't," he assured her. Whereupon she accepted three pieces. Ed watched until she swallowed the last one, then stated ominously, "It does have lard in it."

Sophia let out one bloodcurdling scream, turned, and made a beeline for home, Ed running after her claiming, "No, it doesn't, Sophia—no it doesn't. I was only teasing."

I never did know whether the candy had lard in it. But many emancipated years and miles later I attended a beautiful ceremony, the bar mitzvah of a friend's son. There, in the Jewish synagogue, I made my silent and belated apology to Sophia—for not respecting and not understanding. We didn't know.

For though I lived half my life among them, I never really knew any of these people, my neighbors. My world existed across town where the richer Negroes lived. And if the people around me were poorer than I was, most of those people with whom I associated were richer. All had cars—comparatively rare in my day—many had fine houses, some had maids, and most attended private schools. This didn't bother my mama either. Not because she was not the "keep up with the Joneses" type but because she honestly believed that anything she owned was better than anything anybody else owned—her name, her stove, her icebox. Her family name was unsullied, gas didn't cook as well as wood, and those new electric refrigerators had to be defrosted and poisoned your food.

Anyway, balanced as I was between the two worlds, I somehow got to think of people as people—not white or black or Jews—and when tragedy came I was able to keep that balance.

It came one Christmas Eve night, when I, then a teenager, returned home from a party at one of the big homes across town. Mama and I chattered gaily as we came up the walk. The house was ablaze with lights. Daddy and the boys were perhaps decorating the tree?

Daddy opened the door.

"Don't get excited!" he shouted. *"Don't get excited!"*

So naturally Mama fainted even before she reached the living room, where both my brothers lay bleeding, the doctors gathered around and two policemen. No, I think the policemen came later. It isn't very clear—mostly I remember the blood and that my dress was blue and very beautiful. Everything seemed unreal, and I moved as one in a dream, changed my dress, gave Mama aromatic spirits of ammonia, held a flashlight, and watched through my tears while a doctor sewed up the wounds.

I learned the details later. My brothers had been walking home from work. They both had jobs driving trucks for High's department store. Ed had just finished high school, but there was no money for college that year, so he was working. Sam was out of college, but that was the only job he could get. And late this Christmas Eve, after delivering the last of the packages, they were walking home. I kept thinking, *just walking home from work.* My brothers were good boys—no fights, no squabbles, no trouble. Some white boys were standing around a tavern and jumped them for no reason at all. And this too I kept thinking: no reason—not anger, not robbery, just prejudice. And such a vicious prejudice. They had cut them with switchblades and left them for dead.

But, somehow, ingrained as my mother's philosophy was, this prejudice did not transmit itself to me. These were simply hoodlums. The *white people* were still Mrs. Brookman, Mr.

Smith across the street, the boys' bosses from the store—who all came to bring flowers and candy, tokens of affection. And strange as it may seem, I never heard my brothers mention the boys who did it. Somehow they did not seem important—at least not as individuals. But as symbols of the cruel bigotry and fanaticism under which we lived, the wounds went deep.

It was the scars that bothered Sam. He had several across his face and he would look into the mirror and say, "Now I look like just what they think I am—a good-for-nothing cut-throat. Now I'll never get a decent job." And my mother and father got medicine to put on the scars so they'd fade away; with hardly any money to live on they got medicine for the scars. But I knew the scars were deeper than that.

Past the surface scratches of the hoodlums' switchblades, buried under the sugarcoatings of the Mrs. Brookmans and friendly whites that we knew, were the deep, ugly bruises of a lifetime of blows—the long, long walk on a cold, wintry day to the segregated school, the push to the back of the bus, the climb to the "jim crow" section of the theater to see a special movie, the longing walk past the spacious parks and swimming pools reserved for whites, and his job—truck driver, under the supervision of a man whose education could not touch his own. The switchblade scars were only surface marks—a symbol of "what *they* think I am."

But it was to Mama's credit that what *they* thought we were was no indication of what we thought we were.

Bill and Eva Rutland with first daugher, Elsie, 1945

2
Ready or Not

I do not mean to give the impression that I approved of Mama's slapdash methods of child rearing. In fact, I disapproved quite vociferously.

"Just wait," I told her, "until I have mine. I'll show you how to rear children."

Words I was to eat many years later.

I was a child and I spake as a child. Now that I have become a mama I know better. You don't rear children. They rear you.

As I say, I wasn't trained to be a mama. I wonder if anybody is—reading, writing, arithmetic, Latin, French, Shakespeare, piano lessons, dancing lessons, typing, shorthand, eyelash curling. No help at all when it comes to putting on a diaper.

But who's thinking about diapers? You go blithely along striving to become a witty, charming, intelligent, graceful, beautiful woman. And finally some man discovers this charming you and hastens to make you his. Then right away before you get the orange blossoms out of your hair, you discover that all the charm in the world won't stand up against a burnt roast.

Long before you've mastered the roast you've lost half your charm and all your figure. And one fine day you hear a doctor say, "Congratulations—you have a lovely six-pound girl."

And that's it. Ready or not, you're a mama.

Then you start worrying about the diapers—and that isn't all. Me, I worried about dropping her on the cement floor of our apartment.

Our apartment was at Tuskegee Army Air Force Base. Dear old TAAF. You may not remember way back in World War II when Uncle Sam was scraping the bottom of the barrel and decided to accept Negroes into the Air Force. Of course, integration had not yet become so fashionable. So, on a puddle of mud not too far from where the great Negro philosopher and educator Booker T. Washington had urged the Negroes to "let down your buckets where you are," Uncle Sam quickly erected runways, hangars, barracks, offices, cafeterias, a hospital, and recreation centers; and the first United States Negro Air Force Base came into being. Here the cream of the Negro crop—the healthiest, handsomest, most intelligent brown men ever gathered in one spot—were stationed at TAAF. Of course it did remind me (and forgive the comparison) of what plantation days must have been like—the white master ruling millions of slaves, with a few slaves having the privilege to "blow the whistle." For in charge of all divisions were white majors and captains. The Negro officers were only puppets, second in command.

We were here because my husband was a civilian worker—the only one I know who could outcuss the white major in charge. As my girlfriend would report to me, "Eva, Bill's in the major's office and the cuss words are just a-flying." I worried, of course, but needlessly. Somehow this only endeared and made him indispensable to the major, and he was deferred from military service seven times on account of his job. Of course, he might as well have been in the services. He served throughout the war.

But I am missing my point. What I started to say was that Uncle Sam had erected those apartments for his airmen and civilian workers, and they had cement floors, and I kept thinking, "What if I should drop the baby?" I worried so much I developed a high fever and so delayed my hospital departure for sixteen days.

Finally I could put it off no longer and came home to be a mama. I'll say this for me. I tried. Even Bill admits this. He says he'd come home from the office and I'd have the book in one hand and the baby in the other, and the house looked like you know what. Trouble was, I should have had the book instead of all that Latin and French and such. Or maybe I shouldn't have had the book at all, but I really don't know what I would have done without it. It had a time for everything—bottle, nap, orange juice, water—and believe me my daughter Elsie got nothing that the book didn't say she was to have and not unless it was the time she was supposed to have it.

And the formula. Bill swears I boiled everything in the house that came within hearing distance of the baby and that I locked him and everyone else outside while I, encased in surgeon's gown, cap, and mask, prepared the formula. This is not true. I couldn't find a surgeon's gown.

Now do not be fooled, young mother. You may think that once you have mastered the diapers and the formula, you have the magic secret. Just wait until he begins to talk. And worse still—until he begins to think. And if you're a Negro mother, best you'd been born in my mother's day when you carried your dignity in your heart and not into the five-and-ten, or a few generations from now when everybody will either be brothers or blown to bits. But not now.

Unlike Mama, I had both psychology and integration.

Elsie started thinking out loud about five years and three babies later. The last two were twin girls, only one year younger than their brother. (Can you imagine *three* babies in diapers?) But by that time I had the bathing, bottle, diaper routine under control.

It was the thinking that got me.

Like the time we strolled together one sunny afternoon.

"Oh, Mama," Elsie said, "don't look at those *white peoples!*"

Shocked, I stared at "those white peoples"—a chubby, freckled-faced boy about my daughter's age and his slightly older sister who flashed a toothless, amiable smile in our direction. Grinning back apologetically, I whispered to Elsie, "Why?"

"They're bad."

"You don't even know them."

"But they're white peoples!"

This I was not prepared for. We thought we had kept our frustrations from the children. And that's what we were—frustrated—when all the integration business started.

It started in the armed forces you know. Soon after that presidential proclamation that integrated the armed services, TAAF had to go. We were grateful for the rights and dignity and all but more concerned about our jobs.

The officers and airmen went dutifully and doubtfully to their new posts. The civilians scurried for cover—some to the nearby veterans hospital; some back to their teaching jobs; some, like my husband, followed the boys to Lockbourne, the new base for Negro pilots. When Lockbourne too had to go, Bill was prepared. He had applied and been accepted at Wright Patterson Air Force Base—headquarters—where beat the heart of the Air Force.

It seems so simple. But it wasn't. Housing was limited for Negroes; jobs were limited. One time Bill sat for two weeks in the personnel office at Wright Patterson—his application had not said "Negro," and although that should not have complicated matters, it did.

But these frustrations we had kept from the children. Or so we thought.

And the personal frustrations that might affect them? I had shielded them from as much as I could. And when I couldn't, I had braced myself for the hurt and humiliations. On a visit to Atlanta, I held my breath when Elsie walked up to the burly policeman and asked to blow his whistle, but he merely grinned and explained that only policemen were permitted to blow.

My heart skipped a beat when she tiptoed up and drank thirstily from a fountain marked "White Only"—but the floorwalker smiled and murmured, "cute kid." I lifted a restraining hand when my two-year-old walked up and made friends with a little blue-eyed blonde in a stroller, but her mother only seemed interested in how he had acquired such an extensive vocabulary. No incidents that I could think of. Why, then, this chip-on-the-shoulder attitude? I searched my mind for an answer.

Then it struck me with full force. My five-year-old had started school!

We were living in Xenia, Ohio, then. The town had two elementary schools and two high schools, one of each located in the white section and the other two in our "East End" of town. Theoretically, students for each school were determined by the zone in which they lived. Really, the Negroes went to one school and the whites to the other, zone or no zone. The white schools were beautiful buildings surrounded by shrubbery and grassy lawns, located across the street from the public library and about a block from the community stadium and gymnasium, all of which were easily accessible. The Negro high school was a dismal building on a dismal street. Academically, the white school offered everything from A to Z with all the trimmings while the Negro school was so woefully lacking in subject material that its graduates could hardly pass an entrance examination to a second-rate institution of higher learning.

I had heard resentment before.

From Dean, a charming boy with an exceptionally high IQ who out of his resentment and frustration said, "I can't stand that place (the Negro high school), the children are so dirty"—when what he meant was, "I'd sure like a chance to go to a better school with more challenging subjects."

From Julia, my babysitter: "I don't see why I can't go to the white school. I know how to ignore them when they call me 'nigger.'"

From Edward, another friend, who, although he rated seventh in the county exams, claimed he "would have rated higher except they never give the Negroes a higher rating."

Poor little youngsters—bitter, resentful, envious—none of them really able to define their feelings but all looking with yearning toward that attractive school for the "special set"; a small segment of the millions of brown boys and girls standing in various schoolyards all over the country saying, "I pledge allegiance to the flag of the United States of America, and to the Republic for which it stands, one nation, under God, indivisible, with liberty and justice for all—(but *me*)."

Strangely enough, I felt no inclination to battle the whole problem.

In my selfishness I thought only of Elsie—how to keep her from retaliating with a prejudice of her own, more poisonous and more dangerous to her personality than anything else I could imagine.

But it was Elsie who solved this problem in her own way.

Elsie had a very close, very real relationship with God. How this was acquired in her short span of five and one-half years I do not know.

True, she had been "exposed" to him. We like to think of ourselves as a Christian family, but our attendance at church is irregular, and, although we make a long ritual of prayers on special occasions like Thanksgiving and Easter, on too many weekdays we are apt to have to be reminded to ask a blessing before beginning ravenously on dinner. We take our religion rather too casually, I am afraid, and I think Elsie's close friendship with God developed in spite of rather than because of us.

Elsie had the natural curiosity of any five-and-a-half-year-old, and, although I did my best, it would have taken the combined efforts of Plato and Socrates and a little bit of God himself to satisfy her. With Elsie nothing was objective or way out in space; everything was real and related to Elsie, Mama, or Daddy—as were her questions concerning the propagation of civilization:

"Mama, when all these people die, will God just put some more people down here to live?"

"Well, no," I answered in my groping way. "You see, people are being born every day, just as people die every day. You remember two years ago Billy wasn't born, but now he is here, and there are other little babies being born every day."

Elsie sat bolt upright. "Mama," she said accusingly, "have you got anyone else in your stomach?"

"Oh, no," I answered defensively. I suppose she thought Billy and the twins in a period of two short years was just about enough for me! She relaxed at this answer and was deep in her picture book again, leaving me to explain to the ironing lady why I "dared tell that child the facts of life."

All of her questions concerning God have been as sudden and unpredictable as that. Can God see everybody at the same time? Can he tell when you're good like Santa Claus can? Is he stronger than anybody in the whole world? How does God look?

But I think Elsie's real friendship with God sprang from the incident of the uneaten breakfast.

I had no premonition of its significance when Elsie said to me one day after her kindergarten class, "Mama, the teacher asked me if I ate all my breakfast this morning and I told her yes."

"Oh?" I said vaguely. I was busy with the preparation of lunch and only half noticed the apprehensive glance she gave me. It had completely escaped my memory that in the rush to make the school bus that morning, I had allowed Elsie to dash off with her breakfast half-eaten; now I failed to realize that her timid "yes" to the teacher constituted a downright falsehood. Noting my casual answer, Elsie was able to push the incident to the back of her mind, and no more was said about it at that time.

It was that night that the qualms of conscience really began to pain. With the children tucked snugly in bed and Daddy off to a basketball game, I relaxed in our living room and opened my favorite magazine. The soft voice startled me.

"Mama, I'm scared."

Elsie stood in front of me like a little abandoned waif, barefooted, her pajama coat hanging loosely, a tiny snag in the pocket, much as Peter might have stood after the cock crew thrice.

"Scared of what?" I asked, puzzled.

"I told the teacher I ate all of my breakfast."

The events of the morning came back into focus and I finally got the point. "Well, just tell her tomorrow that you were wrong. She'll understand." I gave her a kiss, thinking that I must remember to mend that snag.

She slowly returned to her room, and I opened my magazine. Before I could decide which story would be first, Elsie returned on the run and threw herself into my arms, sobbing wildly.

"Oh, Mama, I'm scared. God might get me for telling that story."

For the first time I recognized her panic. Here was a soul-stirring crisis in her young life, and I had to gather my inadequate forces to meet it.

"Now, wait," I countered. "Let's not get panicky. Let's sit up and talk this over."

She sat up, wiped her eyes, and fixed them expectantly upon mine.

"You know God is not someone to fear," I said, feeling my way as I talked. "Why, God is just like your Daddy. He loves you. He wants us to be good, and sometimes he might punish us to remind us, but he never wants to hurt us. And if we ever do anything wrong, we tell him we are sorry and he will *forgive* us."

"How do we tell him, Mama?"

"Why, just like you pray each night. You can get down on your knees and tell God anything."

"Well wait, Mama; I'm gonna tell him right now."

My abject young sinner slid off my lap, and on her knees uttered this simple prayer: "Dear God, I'm sorry I told the teacher a story. Please forgive me and I won't do it again."

I relaxed, feeling that I had handled this all right.

Elsie stood up and looked me straight in the eye. "What did God say, Mama?"

I marshaled my forces, breathed a silent prayer for divine guidance, and answered as I thought He would. "He said all right. He knows you are sorry. Just tell Teacher about it tomorrow and try not to do it again."

"Did He forgive me, Mama?"

"Yes, God forgives us any time we ask him."

"Well, I'll tell Teacher tomorrow. Goodnight." And off she went, at peace with her world.

I couldn't read the magazine for wondering whether Teacher would understand.

I could hardly wait for Elsie to return from kindergarten the next day, and, although I didn't want to appear too concerned, I couldn't resist asking, "Did you tell Teacher? What did she say?"

"She said okay. Mama, may I go over to Madelaine's after lunch?"

Well, I had certainly overestimated that crisis, I thought. It wasn't until much later that I realized the far-reaching effects of this incident.

For one thing, Elsie acquired a strict adherence to truth—the whole truth and nothing but the truth, so help her God. It was a good trait—but a little hard for a mere parent to live up to. For instance, Billy, my two-year-old son, had a fanatical love for horses. Searching frantically through his book for a picture of one, he was beginning to fret and whine when he suddenly came across the picture of a zebra.

"There it is! There's horse!" he exclaimed triumphantly.

I, busily engaged in bathing one of the twins, was happy for him. "Yes," I cried, "there's a horse!"

"Oh, Mama!" from Elsie. "You shouldn't tell him that story! You know that's a zebra."

I bowed my head in shame as Billy emphatically defended my stand: "That's horse, Elsie!"

"It's a zebra, Billy."

"A horse! A horse!" Billy stamped his foot and shouted.

Elsie, losing in vehemence if not in fact, vented her rage upon me: "Now, you see, when he grows up, he'll find out you told him a story. You're gonna get in trouble with God!"

But the far greater lesson that Elsie learned from this experience was demonstrated to me as I observed her at play one day. She could imitate everyone at church, from the timid secretary who read the announcements to the austere minister. This particular day, she was on one of her preaching orgies. With Billy sitting cross-legged on the floor, completely fascinated, she stood on a chair, waved her arms and shouted, "You must love God. God loves you. You must be good and do like God wants you to. But if you do act bad, then you just tell God about it and he'll forgive you."

This complete assurance, this security that she feels in knowing God understands and will forgive, has made Him seem more human and close to her: "God knows little children forget sometime, doesn't He, Mama?"

Strangely enough she did not try to take advantage of this fact. She tried very hard to do the right thing and even accepted punishment philosophically: "If you are bad, then God tells your mama or daddy to spank you so you'll remember next time, doesn't He, Mama?"

Don't misunderstand me. Elsie was by no means an angel. She has been known to utter such blasphemies as "I wish God hadn't made you" to Billy, her close companion and archenemy. Indeed, I sometimes wondered if she didn't have more than her share of iniquities.

But she seemed to have found her roots. Life and death alike loomed not too large with her new friend beside her.

I remember very vividly the first time she mentioned death. I was on my knees cleaning the bathtub when Elsie walked in and announced in quiet, solemn tones: "Miss Green is old. Miss Green is gonna die!"

Miss Green was an old woman who lived nearby. I was sure Elsie had got her information from the neighborhood children, who in my opinion had too little respect for the old lady. I thought this was a good time to philosophize.

"We are all going to die," I said.

Elsie howled. "I don't want to die! I don't want Daddy to die—or, or you, or anybody!"

"Why baby, don't take it so hard. Dying isn't so bad. You just go up and live with God."

Elsie howled louder. "I don't want to live with God. I want to stay right here!"

I abandoned philosophy: "All right! All right! Nobody is going to die right now. Let's read about Goldilocks!"

Our next conversation about death was two summers later. The church was only a block from our house. Elsie and several other children sat on the parsonage steps and watched a funeral procession. Elsie came home, eyes stretched wide with excitement.

"Mama, they are going to put him in the ground!"

"Yes, I know."

"Well, how will he get out and go up to live with God?"

"Oh, God will see to that." Remembering our previous conversation about death, I didn't think it wise to distinguish between body and soul.

"I guess maybe God will just come down and get him tonight when nobody is looking," Elsie said.

"I guess so." I was grateful for the explanation.

She was thoughtful. "Mama, I wish I hadn't been born for a long, long time."

"Why?"

"So I wouldn't die for a long, long time."

Then, as if realizing that time of birth gave little indication of time of death, she said: "But we don't know when we will die, do we, Mama?"

"No, we don't."

"Well, I won't worry about that, then. That's God's business."

If only we adults could learn to leave God's business to God!

Yes, Elsie was getting closer to God, in her way, and she was taking me with her. Over my kitchen sink was a calendar adorned with biblical scenes. She inquired about these pictures with the same eagerness she exhibited about her fairy tales. As I read and explained the scenes to her (thank

goodness, an explanation accompanied each picture) I felt a
real nostalgia for the church of my childhood where Jesus
and the little children are depicted on a stained-glass window
that bears my grandmother's name. Its inscription is "Suffer
the little children to come unto me, and forbid them not: for
of such is the kingdom of God." The quiet faith that I felt
then—did I lose it along the way? Or has it remained there
in the background, dusty, like my Bible, but ready when I
need it?

I listened to Elsie's long list of "blesses" with a new toler-
ance. The list extended from Mama and Daddy to the paper-
boy's grandmother. And for fear that she might have
overlooked someone, she would end with "Bless everybody,
everybody in the whole world."

One night she lifted her little brown face to mine and
said, "God blesses white people, too, doesn't he."

It was a statement, not a question, and I was glad. For
now she acquiesced. If he loved them, she would too.

And there was my answer, pure and simple. No psychology, just an old lesson that was taught upon a mountain a long
time ago. I tucked her snugly in bed and silently kissed her
cheek. But my thoughts took wings.

Was this, then, the whole answer to all the bigotry, poli-
tics, despotisms, and war—all the false prejudice man has
conjured against himself?

I reverently reached for my Bible and fervently prayed
that Elsie would hold fast to this wonderful Friend she had
found—this Friend who is stronger than Daddy, knows more
than Santa Claus, and loves her more than Mama.

In the years following this episode I have prayed harder
and harder that my children would hold fast to that Friend.
With me for a mama they need all the friends they can get.

Not that they lack.

Several fringe benefits are attached to being a mama and one of these is children. Naturally I don't mean your children. I mean other people's children—the ones who come to play and stay for dinner, the ones that get five-dollar weekly allowances, the ones that never have to do any work, the ones that stay up and watch television as long as they want to. You know them.

Of course I like other children myself. I started liking them the morning the swings were empty. That was after we moved. We were lucky enough to find a brand-new "built-up-off-the-ground" house in the East End, and we could rent it and get off the highway. After three years in a "flat-on-the-ground" house we were grateful.

It was Sunday morning—one of the first really warm days in early spring, when the sun shines brightest, the grass is greenest, and there is a gentle breeze with a warm, earthy swell that entices you outside.

But no one was enticed.

I glanced up and down the street, out the back door, and furtively through the kitchen window at the swings. They were just standing there, straight and silent—and empty.

I kept telling myself it was because they—the neighbors' children—were at Sunday school, as our four were. But I couldn't be sure. We had been living here for only a few weeks, and I didn't know whether most of the children went to Sunday school regularly or not. I distinctly remembered that the previous Sunday I had washed dishes to the tune of a swing's squeak as one of the neighborhood children waited for ours to return.

Now the swings were silent, and the peace and quiet were most disturbing. I was apprehensive, and to tell the truth, I felt guilty. I felt guilty because I had not invited one neighborhood child to Elsie's birthday party the day before.

Actually, I had no reason to feel guilty. Not a child in the neighborhood was in Elsie's age group. Moreover, I had been warned before we moved in.

"Oh, yes, the house is perfect," I had been told. "And that wonderful, spacious backyard! But, my dear, the children? There are millions of them, you know and with that backyard, and four children of your own, and the swings—well, they'll surround you like bees around honey!"

The prospects were none too bright. I visualized the backyard converted into a football field, the flowers (that I planned to plant as soon as I got around to it) trampled unmercifully, the swings torn down almost before we got them up. A nice yard for the children is one thing, but a community playground is quite another. I hoped I could cope with the situation without hurting anyone's feelings, but I certainly did not want to be imposed on.

So we moved. And the children came. They came in hordes—timidly at first. But our friendly four soon rid them of shyness. With wild enthusiasm they welcomed the strangers into the family circle. Billy brought out his football and basketball and guns. Pat and Ginger, the twins, dragged out dolls and doll buggies. Apples, oranges, carrots, and such were split into a dozen pieces. And the swings squeaked continuously. Soon I was able to distinguish a few familiar faces among the newcomers.

There were Donnie and his gang—the bigger boys—who came to play football and then basketball. My first thoughts were, they're too big, too rough, they have no business in my backyard with the little ones.

But because of the backyard, or maybe because Billy had a basketball and a football, they condescendingly allowed him to tag along. And somehow it did my soul good to see our grubby five-year-old (hitherto hemmed in by the girls) being buffeted and tolerated by the big fellows. He achieved a gruff, boyish swagger and gradually was introduced to baseball, basketball, marbles—all the games that are dear to the heart of a little boy.

There was Duane, about Billy's age, with whom he played cowboys and Indians, quarreled, and fought on his own level—which did much for his self-esteem after a session with the big boys.

There was Carol Ann, chubby and pleasant. She fit right in with Pat and Ginger and introduced them to the delightful uses of good old-fashioned mud. Carol Ann made a congenial wedge between the twins, who had come to lean heavily on each other for companionship. I heard less and less that plaintive "Where are you, Patty-Jo?" (or Ginger), when one was out of the sight of the other. I am indeed grateful to Carol Ann, and I have yet to see mud that can't be washed off.

And then there was Eddie. Eddie was someone special—one of those rare individuals who likes everyone and whom everyone likes. I don't know whether I liked Eddie best because he was the jolliest and the most polite, because he indulged the twins the most, because he played the fairest and was so generous, or because he gave Billy his first job.

The job came about naturally enough. Eddie had a paper route. Billy wanted to go along with him to deliver papers. I agreed, thinking it might be good training for him. And so he accompanied Eddie all week and on Friday turned up with thirty-five cents.

I guess Elsie suffered the most from her new surroundings. The few children she had gone around with in our old neighborhood were girls of her age. So the new environment presented quite a problem to Elsie, who was accustomed to ordering Billy and the twins to another area when her friends came to play. But the problem had its assets. She was learning to adapt herself to youngsters of different ages and to boys. I found her taking more interest in Billy and the twins and actually enjoying herself with them. Furthermore, her own friends were old enough to visit her by themselves. And she would visit them. So she did not lack for companionship.

Now about the birthday party. You can see how it was. It was Elsie's party and would, of course, include only Elsie's friends. But to be on the safe side, I bought extra buns and frankfurters. From conversations around the swings I gathered that news of the party had leaked out, and I figured some of the neighborhood kids would be around.

Elsie's friends arrived in their best party mood—so hilarious and joyful that the games I had planned were not necessary. They took possession of the swings, the balls, the yard. My husband took charge of toasting frankfurters over the outdoor grill, while another mother and I presided over the rest of the refreshments. The party was a great success.

But something was missing. Where were the gate-crashers I had provided for? Where were the neighborhood children who were expected but not invited? I kept looking for someone to turn up, but the street seemed to be deserted.

Then I saw Duane. He was riding his little two-wheel bike, up and down, up and down—glancing toward our yard once or twice.

I rushed to the front porch and called to him. But he didn't hear me. Or did he? Anyway, he didn't answer, and as long as I live, I think I'll remember that proud, forlorn little figure, riding silently up and down, up and down.

That's why my eyes were straining anxiously for a glimpse of some child, any child that sunny Sunday morning. I was afraid the neighborhood children would not come back. And I realized what it would mean if I lost them. Who would teach Billy football and independence? Who would be his buddy? Who would offset the twins' dependence on each other? Who would teach them the blessed art of give and take? I thought I had been kind to the children, lending them our yard and our swings. Now I realized how much more they had to offer, and I wished with all my heart that they would come back.

Duane was the first one I saw. He was sitting on the steps of the house next door. He glanced over.

By this time, our four had returned and the swings were silent no longer. Then I saw Billy wander casually toward Duane. My heart stood still. They seemed to be conversing. Suddenly Billy turned and started toward the swings—and, joy of joys, Duane followed. A few minutes later Eddie sauntered across the lawn and Carol Ann came running up the walk. The children had returned.

I'll make it up to you, I promised silently. We will have other birthday parties, to which you'll all be invited. I'll add a slide, a wading pool, a pup tent; no flower bed will mar your playground. And all I ask in return is your company for my children.

Silence may be golden, but some things are more precious than gold, I reflected as I peeled potatoes and listened to the

sounds outside my kitchen window. To me they spelled con-
tentment: the squish, squish, squish of mud pies, the thump
of a basketball against the side of the house, the childish
laughter—and the squeak, squeak, squeak of the swings.

Billy, Eva, Ginger, Bill, Patty-Jo, and Elsie, Sacramento, California, 1952

3
Westward Ho!

Through the years the sounds change—the click, click of the Ping-Pong ball, the rock of the record player, and the thump, thump, thump of dancing feet.

And the children change.

I often wonder what happened to Eddie and that quiet, peaceful yard up in the east end of Xenia, Ohio—where the colored people lived.

I know what happened to us. We moved to California.

The government decided to decentralize the Air Force. The various branches and divisions were scattered to installations throughout the country.

By this time my husband had proved himself to the point where the executives were vying for him.

"Go with me to Ogden, Utah, Bill." ("For goodness sake, don't go out there—they are very prejudiced, Eva.")

"Come up to Middletown, Pennsylvania." ("Well, not so bad. I lived in Harrisburg not too far away and . . .")

"Out to California with me . . ."

I didn't really care where, knowing that it wouldn't be Atlanta, which I had now begun to think of as heaven.

When you read about the South with its die-hard attitudes a fear stirs within you.

But being there is different.

Visiting in Atlanta, I would go from one spacious home to another—luncheon and bridge during the day, parties at night. Or we would visit the Lincoln Country Club—the Negroes' private club with its own little golf course. Or we would take the children to visit our alma maters and the other surrounding Negro universities, stroll on the beautiful campuses, listen to a lecture, attend a University Players production, walk through the library. How I wished my children could live there, go to school there. How beautiful it seemed— Atlanta, with its ermine-trimmed, diamond-studded, velvety cloak of segregation. How beautiful it seemed as I turned my back upon it and headed West.

Bill went first on a short trip for business and to find us a home. And here was the first indication that the cloak was gone forever. He tells a rollicking tale of his experiences in a white hotel, served by *white* bellboys and *white* waiters, and his searching desperately through the hotel for a black face to direct him to the "colored section" of town. He even wandered to the kitchen, where he was promptly ejected, but not until he had discovered that the cooks were white too, or at least Mexican or Oriental. And when he finally cornered a Negro at the base who had transferred out before him, he learned the astounding truth—*there was no colored section.* The cloak was gone.

But the truth was that this left him rather naked. For he desperately needed a "colored section." The housing official at the base had found houses for his white colleagues with little or no difficulty. Brand-new, better-than-average tract homes with an executive air, boasting of built-in modern appliances and situated near the air base where they worked. And for about $250 down.

But for Bill—nothing.

Bill set out on his own.

We had not planned to buy. Hospitals and doctors (for all their kindness) had left us rather broke.

But renting, he soon found, was an impossibility. As if being colored weren't enough, he also had four children and a dog.

He traveled with the real estate man to outlandish impossibilities, looked through the newspaper ads, lingered longingly over the three-bedroom, two-bath contemporaries—complete with modern electric kitchens, dishwashers, and garbage disposals—that could be handled with a very small down payment. After several rebuffs, he began to look for the "unrestricted" notation and to rely on the real estate man to direct him to where "they will sell to colored."

And more often than not, the house was in an old section that whites were gradually abandoning for the newer, suburban tract houses. They would sell to a Negro because they could sell to no one else—no one for whom the newer suburban houses were also available. Usually the price they asked more than covered the brand-new house they would purchase.

Eventually Bill found one. Not too bad, he assured me, glancing at me anxiously. They will sell it on contract for $1,000 down. We borrowed money on the car for the down payment and headed west.

Sacramento, California—how green, how clean, how wonderful!

The delightful train ride should have given me some indication. Delightful despite being cooped up in a compartment alone with four active youngsters (Bill had driven out
alone with only Spanky, our dog, in our old rattletrap Kaiser).
Well, I wasn't exactly cooped. Half the time I was fishing one
or the other of them out of somebody else's compartment, and
the other half I was herding them all through the heavy rocking doors of the twenty (I know it *was* twenty!) cars that separated us from the diner. These proved to be profitable trips
for the twins and Billy. They flashed their winning smiles and
rolled their big brown eyes and returned each time loaded
with candy bars and bubble gum—courtesy of every passen-
ger within charming distance. They charmed the waiters too!
("Don't bother to come for lunch. We'll bring it to you.") And
when the dining car left us at one point, one of the waiters
brought a big bag of oranges and sandwiches—"Steward
didn't want the kiddies to get hungry."

They charmed the porter too. This one I wished they had
uncharmed. For he became our personal butler and tourist
guide—like when I gazed in awe at the Great Salt Lake.

"Lotta salt," said the porter at my elbow. "Cuts right
through them poles."

"What poles?"

"The ones that hold up the train track. Have to be replaced ever so often—else they'd just give way."

I held my breath to make the train lighter and dared not
ask when was the last replacement.

I marveled at the beauty of the plains, the mountains
rising behind, imagined the pioneers in a circle with their
covered wagons—perhaps Indians descending from the
mountains. I was a pioneer too, I thought. How different
was my journey!

"Hear the clack-clack-clack?" said my porter. "That's a wheel that's worn. Have to report that—sure wouldn't want it to come off."

"Does it ever snow here?" asked Billy.

"Does it ever?" said our porter. "Last year we got snowbound. Couldn't move for four days. No danger. Only thing if we had'a run outa' food and heat. Guess we coulda' froze."

The train wound slowly up the steep mountain. The phrase "men to match my mountains" came to me. The pioneers had to be tough. How could one get a *wagon* over these mountains? How different was our journey.

"Guess he'll make it," came the ominous voice of my porter.

"Who?"

"The engine. Got a lotta cars. Sometimes one engine can't make it up these steep mountains."

A white lady hovered near us in the aisle, but I scarcely noticed. I was pulling the heavy train with all my might.

"What time do we reach San Francisco?" she asked sweetly and politely from the depths of her mink jacket.

"On time!" snapped my porter, and the lady scurried away, rebuffed and uninformed.

"Damn fool question. White folks make me sick," said my porter. "Always asking damn fool questions." And he went on to entertain me with accounts of the "lady that had a heart attack and died, and they had to put her off the train—right there at that shack—right there—on account of you can't keep dead folks on a train."

Somehow, miraculously, we arrived safely. Bill had no trouble locating us, though he started at the wrong end of the twenty cars.

Someone from each coach called out (to the handsome colored gentleman with the worried look), "Are you looking for the lady with the four children?" And they would point "That way."

We were united with our husband and father with the whole train watching, waving, beaming, wishing us well!

That's another thing about being a mama. People notice you.

With the glow of good fellowship from the train ride, we drove through the streets of Sacramento to our new home—how green, how clean, how *uncrowded!* I was so impressed by our own street—a neat, neighborly looking street lined with tall elm trees (I had really expected palms like the ones on my husband's postcards, but elm was good enough)—that I almost forgot my qualms.

Integration qualms, that is. Integration in theory is a fine, high-sounding utopia. In reality I shivered as I watched my children unknowingly shed the warm cloak of segregation, their happy isolation with Eddie, Carol Ann, and all their many Negro friends in the East End.

That's another thing about mamas. We are neither broadminded nor progressive. We just want the children to be happy.

I didn't say anything. You don't, you know, until you have to. Just "Oh, yes, you will like it here. Never mind, there will be other boys and girls to play with." And, "Of course the new teacher will be nice."

And they didn't even notice. Of course, Billy and the twins were too young. But even Elsie didn't notice until that morning when I was brushing her hair. I don't know why Elsie introduces all of her serious conversations when I am brushing her hair, but she does. Almost as if the brush reaches down into the innermost recesses of her brain and releases a tremendous train of thought.

I was brushing vigorously, one eye on the clock and the other on Billy struggling halfheartedly with his shoelaces. Elsie was watching Billy too. He could not go to school unaccompanied, so her movements were somewhat controlled by his.

"Oh, hurry, hurry, Billy, hurry," she begged. "I want to walk to school with Bonnie."

The next door slammed and I glanced apprehensively at Elsie, for this indicated Bonnie's departure. For the moment this escaped Elsie, reminding her only of Bonnie herself.

"That's Bonnie," she beamed and immediately began to chant in a sing-song voice, "Oh, Bonnie, I love you, Bonnie, I love you."

Then, "Why, Mama," she said, "I love a little white girl. I never thought about it. I've been playing and playing. Why, I never even thought about it."

And Elsie was as surprised by the fact that she had never thought about Bonnie's being white as I had been for the past two weeks.

And the neighborhood went on its placid unassuming way, accepting—along with blue-eyed Bonnie, Alfred Shimizu, and Sheri Yee—the new Negro family in the neighborhood.

Only one For Sale sign went up—on the house of the spry little blue-eyed, gray-haired lady two doors away. I sensed that it was because of us and warned the children to be particularly careful to stay off her lawn.

"Don't worry," Billy informed me, wild-eyed. "She's a witch! Jeffrey [the little Italian boy who lived upstairs next door] told me. She poisoned his dog!" Shades of Mrs. Brookman, the witch of my own childhood.

But the twins ignored neighborhood rumors and signs and went on their own inquisitive way, discovered "she ain't a witch—jes Miz Pie and she got candy," and respected my wishes about the lawn, but concluded it was all right to climb into the big armchair with her and listen to fairy tales. And I might have been surprised the day she came down and invited the whole family to dinner—but the twins weren't.

But if the neighbors were nice, the house was impossible.

Well, not really impossible. At first I was impressed—the large living and dining rooms with the solid redwood paneling almost to the beamed ceiling, the lovely stone fireplace and mantle, the big, big yard. All of these features made me praise Bill's choice. And I thought surely we could fix the crumbling walls upstairs, seal up the cracks, get new windows, finish the attic, install a bathroom upstairs, pull out the outmoded plumbing, remodel the present bathroom and kitchen, rewire, reshingle, repaint, and add on a playroom. We even had an architect draw up the plans.

Then came an endless stream of contractors. My spirits (as Patty-Jo would say) went *downer* and *downer*. For as our prospects for a bright, shining remodeled house decreased, our need for it increased—because for some reason, we became alarmingly popular.

The Negro community, scattered though it was, embraced us as one of its own. And, surprisingly, through Bill and his work we accumulated a wide circle of white friends. Imperfect though it may be, there is something about an integrated community. It tends to release the hearts and minds of its people, leaves them free to choose their friends in the light of mutual interests.

Hearts and minds notwithstanding, all this visiting back and forth made me self-conscious. Not only were my white friends better housekeepers than I was (this I do not attribute to the color of their skin—take the Negro family who moved across the street from us who repapered, repainted, spit, polished, and shined their little house before I could say "You think I should wash the windows?") but they had better houses to keep—those gorgeous three-bedroom, two-bath, family-room mansions with dishwashers and garbage disposals that they *could* buy.

And we couldn't. And like I say, my spirits went downer and downer and hit rock bottom the day the Japanese contractor said to me, "Should I tell you the truth?"

"Yes," said I.

"You won't get mad?"

"No."

"You sure you won't get mad?"

"No."

"Well—why *don't you tear this house down and* . . ."

So began the hunt for a new house—and our own private battle against subterfuge. For many subtle ways exist to circumvent the purchase of a house by a Negro. One price is quoted to you, another to a white buyer; your loan doesn't go through—many ways.

Once we thought we had one. Really, I didn't like it. It was a multicolored brick monstrosity.

My husband was enraged.

"Why *don't* you like it?" he stormed.

"Too small."

"It has four bedrooms."

"Like closets."

"And a family room."

"Just an extension of the kitchen. I could never get away from the children."

"Two bathrooms."

"I know."

"And built-ins, and a big yard."

"I know."

"And *they will sell it to us.*"

This I couldn't beat. We signed the papers and paid the deposit. On the way home my husband sighed. "You know, I don't like that house either." We consoled each other.

"We can extend the family room."

"Paint the brick."

"At least it's new."

Next morning the phone rang. Our agent was most apologetic. The owner wanted $26,000 instead of the quoted $22,000, and he wanted cash (although it already had an $18,000 insurance loan against it). I recognized the subterfuge, but I could have kissed him.

Hooray for discrimination! We didn't have to buy the brick monstrosity.

Happily clutching the returned deposit check, we resolved from then on to make no compromises. Nothing that we didn't want just because we could buy it.

Failing in all efforts to buy, we decided to build. Not that a lot was easier to buy than a house. I searched and found a lovely corner lot with a big oak tree.

"I couldn't touch it," said my Negro agent.

I got on the phone (Bill was out of town and this was a good buy) and called one of our white friends.

"I've found a lot. Will you buy it for me?"

He didn't hesitate. "Of course."

It still wasn't easy—finding a contractor who would build for us, getting a loan. Nor was it pleasant.

Our white friend was called. How dare he sell to a "nigger"? "Will you be happy," asked a casual white acquaintance, "knowing they don't want you?"

But I was emancipated. I had picnicked in the public parks, played golf on the public fairways, taken the children to the public integrated dancing classes, lived on a lovely shaded, integrated street. I had tasted the fruit of full citizenship (well, nearly full) and found it delicious. Remembering the east end of Xenia and the slums of Atlanta, I shed once and for all the stifling cloak of segregation.

"It is where I want to be," I answered.

"But the children . . ." she persisted.

I smiled. "They'll survive."

And grow I thought to myself. I had not forgotten the vulnerability of their position. But this I had learned to accept and strangely enough to appreciate. For I remembered Janey and that day she didn't come.

That day, Elsie pressed her little face against the window eagerly, expectantly—and my heart turned over.

How could I explain? What could I do? It's something you always think you're prepared for, but you know you'll never be really prepared. You just hope you can handle it to soften the blow.

"Elsie," I said, "she may not come, you know."

Elsie turned on me indignantly. "She said she would. She said so. She said her mother saw me at school one day and that I was clean and neat, not like . . . not like . . . well, you know."

I knew what she meant.

That was the day she had come home screaming, "This house is so dirty."

She had a point, I thought, as I collected the books and crayons and rescued the cracker box from one of the twins.

"Not dirty, just a little cluttered," I defended myself.

"Dirty, dirty, that's what Janey's mother said. She said Negroes were all dirty and they kept dirty houses, and Janey can't play with me, even at school she can't, and she can't come over and . . ."

"Well," I hesitated. What could I, the world's worst house-keeper, say to that? "That's not true. Our house isn't really *dirty* and neither are . . ." I mentioned a few of our friends who were immaculate housekeepers.

I wondered later why I was defending myself. Why should I try to prove to my own daughter that we were as good as any-one else and solely through the automatic, superficial process of keeping our faces and houses clean, of putting up a front? What of our hearts and minds? I determined the next time the subject came up I would place it on a higher plane.

I looked at Elsie leaning against the window and thought of what Janey had done to her in the past few months. And not intentionally—at least I don't think it was intentional. Little children aren't clever enough to be *that* cruel.

For every day at school she would play with Elsie, and every day she would walk home with her as far as a certain corner, where she would turn off because her mother might see her. And her mother didn't allow her to play with Negroes because "Negroes were dirty. Negroes were loud and uncouth. Negroes can't be trusted," et cetera—all explained in exquisite detail to Elsie. Every day Elsie would come home crying and Billy would explain, "Janey's been talking about colored people again."

Now Elsie stood against the window. (No, no jeans today; she had to remain neat, *please*. And "Billy, get your crayons up, please.") Neat, clean, ready for inspection.

"Oh, Janey, please come," I implored. "Please let her," I asked Janey's mother. And my heart ached for the neat girl, still in school clothes, leaning against the window—a tiny paragon of virtue, a defense for the whole Negro race, a battalion ready to batter down all the bigotry and stupidity ground into Janey's mother for two centuries. She looked so little, so defenseless.

What do you say? Where was all my big talk?

"Come help me peel the potatoes," I said, "She may come later." Elsie turned from the window. She too knew that Janey would not come.

"What did you do at school today?" I asked, to divert her. But she was not to be diverted.

"Janey says Negroes shouldn't be in this neighborhood, anyway. Her mother is very careful about her. She can't play with Chinese or Negroes or . . ." Here the bottled-up tears spilled over, and she cried plaintively, "Oh, I wish I wasn't colored!"

"Elsie," I said, "don't, don't ever say that!"

"But, I do, I do!" she screamed. "I hate Janey!"

No, I thought, please, Janey, don't infect Elsie.

"Elsie, listen to me," I implored. "You mustn't hate Janey. Just feel sorry for her. Her mother isn't very understanding. She doesn't know the real values. She doesn't yet know how to judge people on their character, so she bases her judgment on false values like color of skin or cash in their pockets or something like that. Do you see?"

"Yes, I see," she said.

Then, "Mama, who can't I play with?"

"Why, Elsie," I answered, "you can play with anybody."

"*Anybody?* You mean real black people too?"

"Anybody," I said firmly.

"Oh, Mama," she asked, anxiously, "aren't there maybe some Indians that don't speak English that I couldn't play with?"

I folded her in my arms then, and my tears came too.

"Oh, Elsie, baby, look. You mustn't be silly because other people are. That isn't the American way. We judge people by the kind of people they are inside, whether they are kind and good, not how they look or speak."

"But Janey's an American, and her mother doesn't let her play with me."

"Well, Elsie," I said, "that's her business. People have the privilege of choosing their associates. But all people are not like that. Bonnie is white, and she is one of your best friends. And I hope you'll be more intelligent about the way you choose your friends. And, Elsie, even if Janey's mother doesn't like you, she can't stop you from living in this neighborhood or going to the public school because you are entitled to all the privileges any other little American enjoys. The laws of this country say so. But you'll just have to be patient with people like Janey's mother. It's just that their hearts and minds haven't quite grown up to the laws they've made."

I hoped she understood. I couldn't be sure. I cuddled her, I wiped her tears, and presently she put on her jeans and went outside. I could only hope.

It wasn't until two years later that I realized how well she did understand. It was across the country, in another city, and I was chattering gaily with a friend whom we were visiting. Elsie, inconspicuously nearby, munched on an apple.

My friend, a teacher, was discussing her work—teachers, children, attitudes. She dwelled particularly on a colleague of hers, a teacher who was inclined to be partial.

"It's a shame," she said, "how she caters to the children of professionals. If it's a doctor's son, or a lawyer's—he's got it made in her class." She broke off to go into another room for something.

"Gee, Mama," said Elsie, taking a huge bite of apple, "that teacher's not very intelligent, is she? She doesn't know how to judge people by their insides, does she?"

I couldn't speak. I could only shake my head emphatically.

But—"*Thank you, Janey,*" I whispered to myself. "Thank you for helping Elsie to grow in wisdom and understanding and appreciation of her fellow man."

The children would survive the new neighborhood, I thought. And learn and grow.

Only two things bothered me about the new setup. Bright, shiny, new, executive-type houses require cleaning too. And three bathrooms are no guarantee of privacy.

Bill Rutland with coworkers at McClellan Air Force Base, Sacramento, 1954

4
Trouble with Papa

Another trouble with being a mama is papas.
Strike that.

What I mean is one of the *blessings* of being a mama is papas.

The trouble is most papas are people—men. Some papas are papas. I know because I read about them in novels and look at *Father Knows Best* on TV. And only this morning in the lovelorn column (I always read the lovelorns—makes me appreciate my mundane dishes, algebra, and "where's my socks?" routine), I read a letter from a happy, appreciative woman whose husband is a real papa, and I quote: "He never speaks crossly to me and never denies me or the children anything we ask for if he can possibly get it. He always kisses me on returning and leaving home. When he is off work he spends his time at home, follows me around the house, and seems never too tired to give me a hand at anything I am doing. He doesn't loaf on the corner with the boys or play pool or poker, but he does love to take the children and me to the mountains and just walk around admiring the trees and wild flowers and animals. He is never too tired to let the children romp over him awhile, doesn't drink, smoke, or use bad language, and we always talk over our problems quietly."

Quietly.

Well.

All I've got to say is it's a good thing that lady knows how lucky she is, because if she didn't, I could tell her a few things. Like *papas are not quiet.*

They roar.

At least our papa does. He roars when the house is not clean, when he can't find his socks, when dinner's not ready, when somebody's algebra teacher just phoned, when somebody's been fooling with his razor, and, "*Isn't anything sacred around here?*"

He roars at report card time, when somebody hasn't come in yet and if they are not splattered on some highway he's going to kill 'em when they do get in, when somebody's lost his golf balls, and, "*Isn't anything sacred around here?*"

He roars when Billy's still got that cold and blast it no, he's not going to that football game, when Billy got spiked and how in tarnation did that happen and how come that idiot coach doesn't know how to apply a bandage, when Billy won't keep off that blasted foot like he jolly well told him to, when somebody uses bad language, when he still can't find his socks, and, "*Isn't anything sacred . . .*"

What really gets me, and I hate to admit it, is that this roaring gets results. One quick hearty roar from Bill accomplishes more than a thousand "darling, will you pleases" from me. I don't know why, but when he's home, miraculously the grass gets cut, socks get picked up, lessons get done, and dishes get washed. And another thing: *nobody* roars back.

As a matter of fact, the children and Papa seem to have reached some sort of understanding.

For instance, take the other day, when after three days of "darlings, will you pleases" I finally prevailed upon Bill to urge the twins to clean their room.

Result: much roaring and stirring as if a tornado were tearing through that part of the house. I could not help but catch brief snatches of the repartee.

Bill: "You'd just better get in here and get this disgusting mess cleared up or I'm going to take it out of your ornery hides!"

Loud laughter from Patty-Jo, who would laugh on the way to her own funeral: "Daddy, you sound so funny."

"You're gonna look funny if you don't get this—what in blue blazes are you keeping *this* in here for?"

Another gay reply, whereupon Bill asserts: "If you don't clean out this drawer and shut your mouth I'm gonna put my foot in it."

Pat: "You couldn't get your foot in my mouth!"

Bill: "I bet if you opened it wide enough I could."

Hysterics from Pat.

After much roaring, cursing, et cetera, Pat comes through the kitchen to carry out the trash and says to me, "Gee, Mom, I like for Dad to help us clean out our room. He's much more fun than you."

He's much more fun than me at cards too. And Ping-Pong, Scrabble, Monopoly, baseball, high jumping, swimming, or practically anything the family might participate in. And this I really cannot understand because he fusses, squabbles, cheats, and yells as much as the kids do.

So then I comfort myself with the thought that all right if he is more fun than me he's also more *honest* than me. And that's bad. At least it is if you are interested in children and protecting their egos. You have to lie (a little). That is, you might call it lying. I call it *tact*.

"Do you think this makes me look too skinny?" Elsie asks.

"Of course not," I reply. "It fits you nicely. You just have a dainty figure."

"Great Caesar," Bill explodes, "what are you wearing that for? You look like a toothpick."

"Gee, I wanted to get picked for varsity," Billy will say.

"Well," say I, "don't be discouraged. This is your first year. I'm sure you are just as good as that what's-his-name they picked instead of you."

"For the love of heaven," says Bill. "You don't get *picked* for varsity. You *make* it. And don't you forget it. You have to pro- duce. You gotta *be* there and you gotta *produce*. Now let's see— you missed practice that time, and remember that basket you didn't make . . ."

"Ginger, darling," I say, "do you think you should have so many potatoes? You want to preserve your figure, you know."

"Preserve it!" roars Bill. "You've got too much of it now. Get those potatoes off your plate, you big fat slob."

You see?

No attempt to preserve their darling vulnerable egos. I keep telling him and telling him.

Anyway, what really gets me is when the girls ask for my *honest* opinion on some outfit and I say, "Oh, it's beautiful on you," and *they* say, "Gee, I wish Daddy were here. *He'd* tell me." And Billy never seems to care whether I'm on the side- lines at basketball or baseball or anything else. But when a *big* game is coming up he always asks, "Dad, will *you* be there?"

Almost as if they *like* their egos smashed.

And that's the way papas are—hard as a rock on their families and boys that are taking their daughters out, soft as a jellyfish where other people are concerned.

"Hello, Mama," he will say on the telephone ten minutes before dinner, "There are a couple of fellows up from Pasadena, and I'm bringing them home for dinner."

Or, as he walks in the door, "Hi, Mama, this is Major Igbaul and Captain Khan from India. They're attending a session here, and I brought them home for dinner and bridge."

I hate to admit it, but often these impromptu inconveniences prove more profitable to me than to the guests. Igbaul and Khan had us over to their apartment one evening and served us a real Indian meal: curried chicken, curried beef, and such a clever salad arrangement—tomatoes, celery, thin slices of cucumbers, temptingly sprinkled with what I thought was paprika and discovered, too late, was hot pepper!

We had an interesting conversation too. It seemed one of them, not being used to an alarm clock, had difficulty getting up in the morning.

"How do you get up at home?" I asked.

"Oh," he said, "my man wakes me when he brings my newspaper and hot tea."

My envious look must have prompted his next lines, for he spoke admiringly about my modern household gadgets.

But it somehow seems to me that a servant gently nudging me in the morning to present a hot cup of tea and a newspaper has a dishwasher beat all to pieces!

Anyway, Bill's visitors keep coming.

Lee Tsu, the visitor from Taiwan, taught me to cook vegetables the Chinese way.

And Mr. Jones. "Mama, here's that guy from Japan. He was so nice to me, and he's been transferred out here, and they haven't found a place yet and so . . ."

My mind begins to rearrange children and count sheets as Bill ushers in Mr. Jones, his Japanese wife, two children, two cats, one dog, and five suitcases, beginning a hectic week that disturbs my benevolent husband not at all, as he has my mama's "we've got it, he needs it, so give it to him" philosophy. However, it has always been rather hard on me, being more of the "Sunday morning" type Christian and of the "we need it, so let's keep it" philosophy.

Like my mother, Bill is the cheerful, sweet, "you are eager to please him" type.

Now this works out very well in Bill's profession. And I'd like to tell you about his profession, but this isn't easy.

When I mention casually that my husband brought the "beautiful" dress from Paris or that Bill is in Germany or that last year he took a jaunt around the world or that he brought me china from Japan, people stare at me and say, "What does your husband do?"

And I'm hard pressed to tell them.

"He works for the government," I answer lamely.

"I know. But what is his title?" Or as a friend's child put it the other day, "I mean, what is he? you know, like a doctor or a plumber?"

"Well, he is a program engineer," I say.

"Oh, in the *services*," say my friends, and "What is *that?*" says the child.

"No," say I, "he's not in the services." And to the child, "Well, you see he has something to do with airplanes and government missiles."

"Oh, he builds them," says the child.

"No, he *talks* about them," say I, "to people who are going to build them or going to buy them or going to borrow them—about how much and how many and how long and who's going to do what—in meetings all over the world."

I'm hard pressed explaining to others too—like on school or credit applications. His title is always changing, so I put program engineer, projects officer, logistics officer, et cetera, and go through the same routine of explaining.

One day when Bill was with me and filling out some forms, I leaned over to see what he put on the application so that the clerk didn't look aghast and the questions didn't begin.

It was "government clerk."

Anyway, in his profession, his charm serves him well. Secretaries cheerfully arrange his itinerary and get the tickets, cars meet him, the elderly German couple he meets on a train invite him to dinner, the angry men at the conference table warm to his humor and reach an amicable decision (once he broke a deadlock by remarking to all the white faces around him, "There's a 'nigger' in the woodpile, and I know it ain't me"), and despite the white colonel's admonition to "let me do most of the talking—these people have no respect for the American Negroes who allowed themselves to be enslaved," the Ethiopian general defers to "Mr. Rutland" on every important point and there seems to be a feeling of kinship between them.

He charms his family too. Only in our case, we not only want to please him, we just darn well *better* please him.

But somehow we don't mind. Despite my leanings to the contrary, way down deep inside I like a spic-and-span house with socks in the proper place. And, as I said—when he is home, lessons get done, grass gets cut, children *mind.*

And, as Patty-Jo remarked the other day, "If I ever get in any real trouble, I'm gonna tell Daddy, cause all Mama will say is 'Darling, I forgive you.' Daddy will *do* something."

But it's hard sometimes. Like tonight. I wish I could just disappear. It's report card time, and I tell you I'm right glad I'm not bringing one home.

Speaking of report cards reminds me of one outsider whom Bill was hard on—James Meredith.

When the rumor—and I'm everlastingly glad it was just a rumor—came out in the press that James Meredith had flunked out and would have to leave the University of Mississippi, I thought Bill would have apoplexy.

It started out innocently enough—small talk at the dinner table. "Gee," says Elsie, "the paper says Meredith will have to leave Mississippi on account of his grades."

"There's no excuse under God's heaven for it," says Bill, "the low-down, lazy, good-for-nothing . . ."

"Now, just a minute," say I, "give credit where credit is due. He risked his life."

"And two men lost theirs to get him in. And the whole United States Army was behind him. He's got no *right* to flunk out!"

"*Everybody* can't get straight As," says Ginger.

My husband gets louder. "Not asking for straight As. A simple C will keep you in. A nigger can't *afford* to fail."

"He's got as much right as a white man," say I. "They say Mississippi's just a good-time school for those who can't make it anywhere else."

"A nigger's got no right to fail!" At this he jumps up and pounds the table and turns on Billy. "And don't you forget it. If you bring me any more Ds, I'll knock your cotton-pickin'..."

And we quiet down as Papa roars. (And thank you, Mr. Meredith, for not flunking out.)

Later he roars privately to me.

"Don't you dare plant the idea in my children that it's all right to fail. A nigger's *got to win.* He's got to be on top."

Then I remember.

I remember that it is he who is facing the outside world. And I remember that it was not and is not always a charming, glamorous world.

I remember the time he sat two weeks in a personnel office because the job he had been given through correspondence "might not be the one for you" when the real reason was "we don't have Negroes in this capacity, supervising so many whites." I remember that the situation was saved by a man setting up a new section, a man who so desperately wanted a man with Bill's capabilities that color didn't matter.

I remember the promotions he didn't get. "You know, there's quite a bit of public relations involved, a white man might be better." I remember one time when a buddy whom he had trained got the promotion. It was the buddy who said, "You're the best man. I just got it because I am white."

I remember that it was with respect for his capabilities that the Ethiopian general deferred to "Mr. Rutland."

I remember the hotel clerk who hesitated about reservations until Bill gave his name. Then she said, with respect, "Oh, you're Mr. Rutland who's running the conference. There have been several phone messages."

I remember the reservation he didn't get—at a government school in Washington, DC. "Some mistake, some mix-up, no room for you." He had to take two streetcars and a bus from my aunt's house while his white classmates simply came downstairs to class. One of them asked, "Hey, aren't you the fellow who's supposed to be my roommate?"

Incidentally, this was a school for training in diplomatic relations—how to spread the democratic ideal abroad—with stock answers for questions such as, "What about the racial situation in the United States?"

When this particular question came up in class, my husband, the only Negro, said, "I was asked this same question by a group of women at an airport in Pakistan. They had mistaken me for an Indian, but finding that I was an American Negro on my way home, they were shocked and unbelieving.

"'You're going *back?*' they asked.

"'Yes,' I replied.

"'You're going back *there?*' they asked incredulously, showing an Indian newspaper with a headline about (and a picture of) Negro students being arrested in a sit-down strike in Nashville, Tennessee.

"'Why are you going back?' they asked.

"'Because it *is* a real picture,' I said. 'Because, despite the inequities, people can sit down or stand up for their rights and for a democratic ideal. And because it is not the *total* picture; because I have a wife and children there; because I have a beautiful home, a good job, and I am respected in my community; because my family and I are well fed and happy; because I can be whatever I want if I work hard enough.'"

He did not say to them as he has often said to me after a jaunt in an underprivileged country, "I'd rather be a *nigger* in *jail* in *Georgia.*"

After Bill returned home from this particular school, he received a letter from a high official apologizing for the "no room" incident and a promise that it "will not happen again." Another door opened.

I remember the time in a borderline town when he and a white buddy entered a cafeteria and Bill was turned away. I remember that my husband was calm and dignified, that it was the buddy who raved, a man who was seeing discrimination personally for the first time in his life and became, as Bill said, "another converted white man."

I remember the conference in Kentucky that Bill conducted with a leading airplane production company and the elaborate luncheon the company had arranged for in advance, fifteen men seated at the dining table. All received menus except Bill. Bill, absorbed in conversation, hardly noticed. Then, as the others began to order, he asked the waitress quietly for a menu.

Then came the always shocking, no matter how many times you hear it, "I'm sorry, I can't serve you."

But this time from the company representative comes "What's the matter, Bill?" his indignation, the hurried consultation with the manager who babbles about policy, precedent. *This* time fifteen men arise and walk out, fifteen men representing a powerful company that sustains that town. And as they watch them go, the waitress and the manager are a little disconcerted, as people always are when discrimination affects their bread and butter. You get the feeling it won't happen again. And you are a little thrilled that the capable Negro man who has helped to open another door is your husband.

And, if you are that man's wife, you begin to understand why he roars—what he is saying to your children. It is "I love you. I want you to be happy, to be respected."

The age-old cry of the Negro father; the slave that bowed and toiled and did the white man's bidding that his little brown babies might eat; the newly freed black man who waited tables and carried bags that his child might be educated; a little further up the ladder, the teachers and preachers who planted a dignity, an idea—to stand up, Black Boy, be proud and walk straight, straight into the doors of the universities of Mississippi and Georgia, to the front of the bus, to anywhere you want to go!

I know at last what my husband is roaring about. "The doors are open. Be ready."

And I am proud and happy and thrilled that he is helping to open them. I relax and smile and listen to him roar, and I sort out socks and polish the floor, put a log on the fire, a pie in the oven—and wait and thrill to the key in the lock, the quick masculine step, and the inevitable heartwarming *first* roar: "*Where's your Mama?*"

Ginger, Billy, and Patty-Jo with neighborhood friend,

Sacramento, 1953

5

You Have to Join

Another thing about being a mama is you have to join. And while I'm on this point, I'd like to ask Mr. *Where Did You Go? Out. What Did You Do? Nothing* Smith one question. And that is, "What can you do about it, anyway?" I'm all for kids lying on the ground and looking at the sky and making their own rules and excluding grownups, especially excluding grownups, because all these organizations for the spiritual, moral, and cultural development of youth take a mite of spiritual, moral, and cultural energy—and by that I mean Mama's energy.

Take me.

I started joining as soon as I reached California. With integrated schools and all, one felt one should, well, integrate. And I want to point out here and now, with all the disadvantages being bandied about, that there are some distinct advantages to being colored. And not the least of these is the fact that you stand out in a crowd. Take the first time I attended a PTA meeting. They were having a clothes closet drive. Clothes closet is a pool of used clothing maintained by the PTA for needy children. "We need all types of clothes," the lady stated, but she stressed the fact that they must be *clean*. Thinking of all those woolen jumpers and snowsuits lying abandoned in the attic and clutching in my hot hand the two dollars to get my husband's suit from the cleaner's, I stood up without thinking.

And that's where I had the advantage. For immediately there was a dead silence. How I pitied the other women in that room. Any one of them might have stood up and never been noticed—lost forever in a mass of white faces. But *I, I* commanded immediate attention—I was that *colored* woman. See, over there in that red dress; whatever is she going to say?

What I said was, "What if you have used clothes but can't afford to get them cleaned?"

There came an immediate round of applause. Not only was I colored, I was intelligent, and moreover, I had asked a question that was on the tip of every tongue. And I gained immortality. For three years later when the same thing was mentioned someone said, "Eva, do you remember the PTA meeting when you . . ." See what I mean? Any other woman in that room could have asked, and three years later she would have been a lady who asked! However, I hasten to add that this is a day that seems to be passing. More and more colored women are taking their place in community affairs, and it's getting so you hardly stand out at all anymore.

Ah, well, be that as it may, this is when I became a joiner. I rapidly moved up in PTA circles and other circles—like a good mama should.

I've sold hot dogs, clowned, and blown up balloons at school carnivals. I've collected old clothes; I've made costumes and candy. I've carved soap and made earrings with Cub Scouts, sewed on sequins with Brownies, sold cookies with Girl Scouts. I've learned the Cub Scout Promise, the

Girl Scout Oath, and the Boy Scout Oath. I've sewed on merit badges and Little League numbers. I've been a PTA president, vice-president, program chairman, education chairman, parent education chairman, character education chairman, founder's day chairman, and corresponding secretary. I've sold soft drinks at the Little League stand and carried snacks to Red's Plumbing, Philly's Telephone Answering Service, and at least one other Little League team whose name escapes me at the moment. I've planted poppies with the Girl Scouts, taught Sunday school, fixed a million potluck dishes, suffered through a thousand pack meetings and five hundred Girl Scout picnics, shouted myself hoarse at one hundred and fifty Little League games, and chauffeured a million kids a quarter of a million miles in my day. Let me tell you, I've been a *good* mother up to here!

And it bothers me that all I've got to show for it are four frustrated, nervous youngsters; a mismanaged, ill-kept house; and a husband, *I think.*

Which brings me back to another trouble about being a mama—papas. Papas don't understand. They think food and clean socks and housecleaning take precedence over moral, spiritual, and cultural development any day. I hasten to note that some women can do both. But I'm not one of them.

In the first place, thanks to my mother's slapdash training, I just wasn't equipped for a place-for-everything, everything-in-its-place kind of operation. In Mama's house, you never knew where anything belonged, but if you were looking for something you looked first behind the trunk in her room. "The dirt will be here when I'm gone," said Mama, "and I don't intend to let it rush me." Her method of housekeeping was to fan a feather duster and pull down the shades. She always remembered flowers, though. Even now I can remember coming into a quiet, cool house, a fresh bowl of flowers on the bookcase in the hall, and the sun filtering softly through the yellow shades of the dining room window. You had the illusion of peace and quiet order.

But not me. Lacking both my mama's clever camouflage techniques and my mother-in-law's spit and polish, I'm lost. I don't even have sense enough to fan a feather duster and throw everything behind the trunk. Besides, I don't have a trunk.

But I'm dedicated. To moral, spiritual, and cultural development, that is.

I got so I could walk out of a houseful of unmade beds and dirty dishes to a 9:30 parent education class and not bat an eyelash when the lady next to me thanked goodness she got finished with the vacuuming and dusting before she left home.

That is because I thought it was important—for the kids I mean. Not to escape the dishes, as my husband claims. For by the time the children reached school age, I had conceded that I knew nothing, absolutely nothing, about rearing children, and I was grasping at any straw. How was I to know that I was about six years too late? That it started in the cradle and Elsie was forever doomed to insecurity because she was born in that era of a bottle at six, orange juice at eight, nap at nine, and no petting and no nonsense about it? And that Billy's chronic thumb sucking was the result of the early birth of the twins and bottle feeding? Oh, I learned other things that could be presently applied, I suppose, like speaking quietly produces quiet cooperation—in most families that is. But in mine—conditioned to ear-splitting acoustics as it was—you just didn't get heard. And that order can be produced by an each child's-place-for-everything, everything-in-its-place operation. But after six sessions I knew that my poor children were doomed. I was hopelessly inadequate. Now, if anybody mentions child rearing classes, I just tell them I already don't rear them as well as I know how.

But I didn't stop joining. In an effort to overcome my own inadequacies, I joined—we joined—every "for the good of youth" organization that came along. Which brings to mind another trouble with being a mama—money! And I don't mean "bread and butter and school clothes" money. I mean "joining and belonging" money. And let me tell you that ain't hay.

Take the week my twins "flew up" (from Brownies to Girl Scouts with a real impressive ceremony): two uniforms, $6.50 each; two ties, 60¢ each; two belts, 50¢ each; two anklets, 50¢ each; two caps, $1.50 each; two handbooks, $1.00 each; $1.00 for troop insurance and $1.00 joining fee for each girl. That came to $12.60 for each girl, or—in my case of doubles— $25.20.

It so happened (as it frequently does in my case) that my boy joined the Boy Scouts *the same week,* itemized as follows: initial joining fee, $3.00; registration fee, 50¢; insurance, $1.00; pants, $4.25; shirt, $3.35; belt, 60¢; hat, $1.15; scarf, 55¢; pack rack, $5.95; pack, $3.45; cooking kit, $2.75; bedroll (the cheapest—so cheap that when any of the kids go camping they always insist on borrowing a neighbor's), $11.95. Total: $38.50. Now each boy is supposed to earn his own equipment money. But at eleven years old, that usually means from you.

My oldest daughter came cheap that week—only $2.00 registration fee and insurance, which didn't make much difference because by that time the grocery money was shot anyway.

Please note that no child is disqualified because he can't buy a uniform. The school maintains clothes closets, but these are for the needy. Not for average "middle class on the verge of bankruptcy" families like mine.

My time reached the bankruptcy state too. That year I was president of the PTA. That entailed at least four meetings per month—PTA board meeting, PTA meeting, council meeting, district meeting, not to mention various committee meetings. I was also a den mother—I admit, a bad one. Once a week I corralled eight active youngsters and sat them down to some project that neither they nor I cared about, but we tried to follow the theme. Same thing for Brownies (I was assistant leader). And, oh, yes, I mustn't forget the Brownie leader and den mother training sessions that I had to attend to learn the songs, games, crafts, and ceremonies. Do you wonder that this was the year I almost lost my husband?

But it's worth it, you say. All that spiritual, moral, cultural development.

Well now, I wonder. Maybe I can't speak very loudly, maybe I wasn't a good joiner, and maybe my youngsters are not typical. But, frankly, what mine got *wasn't* worth it.

In the first place, the moral, spiritual endeavors have given over to crafts, picnics, and potlucks—to a frightening degree. For instance, one leading Scout troop in our city has done a most impressive job of making Indian costumes and learning Indian dances—which is fine if they're all growing up to be Indians. But I attended a Boy Scout meeting recently and a visiting leader asked the question about the knot in the Boy Scout neckerchief. Not a boy in the room—and some had been Scouts for two years—knew that it shouldn't be tied until he had done his good deed that day. And a man from the Youth Authority who spoke at our PTA meeting one day indicated an amazingly little difference in the proportion of Sunday school goers and non–Sunday school goers among kids who got into trouble. He frankly admitted he did not know why this was so but suggested that crafts and picture coloring might have replaced stress on the Bible and moral values.

And I might add that it could be because Mama is out attending meetings to train for her diversified role. And it's questionable about how much good the meetings are.

Take the high school board incident a couple of years ago. It was election time and several burning issues were on the ballot that vitally affected the schools. When the legislative chairman asked what she should say about the ballot she was cautioned just to urge the people to vote and for goodness sake don't mention the issues that were too controversial and might spoil the board meeting.

I took issue with this position, rather vociferously, I'm afraid. Made quite a speech about after all *what was the school board for?* Everyone appeared spellbound by my speech—or so I thought. But when the motion (not to take any position or even to permit any discussion of the issues) came to a vote, mine was the only nay. I was disheartened by this, but not nearly so disheartened as when I learned later that several felt as I did but were afraid to take a stand.

This came out when I telephoned individual board members later to notify them of another meeting (I was corresponding secretary with this responsibility) and got the following reactions.

"I was so glad you spoke out at the board meeting the other day." "I do feel we emphasize the wrong things." "Keep it up, girl—lots of us are behind you."

Behind me—but not with me. And it takes more than one person to buck the tea-party trend and get down to the nitty

gritty—the real and not always pleasant things that really affect the children.

Some of them, of course, missed what I was trying to say
entirely. And this is another trouble with being a *colored*
mama. People sometimes think that you cannot think beyond
the racial problem.

For example, "Did someone offend you," asked one member, "at the board meeting the other day?"

I went to great lengths to explain this was not a personal
issue—that I was talking about something bigger than me.

"Oh, I'm so glad," she said, "you see we knew you at the
elementary school but . . ." And she went on and on until I
could see it was no use. She missed the point entirely.

And I was sorry. I have attended two state PTA conventions and have been so inspired to see *all those people* filling to
the rafters the city auditorium—all sincere, dedicated women.
But dedicated to what? Council luncheons, potlucks, and
school carnivals—avoiding the vital controversial issues that
might determine our children's future?

I don't mean to say the PTA does no good at all.

After all, the kids always enjoy the carnivals to raise the
money to send the mamas to the conventions, and the mamas
always enjoy the convention away from the kids. (The only
time I ever got away from *my* husband and kids was the time
I was a delegate to the convention.) Then the PTA sponsors
those wonderful "meet the teachers—know your school"
nights.

In our school system somebody hit upon a perfectly mar-
velous idea for the "know your school" program—so mar-
velous that they're using it over and over again and it's about
to wear me to a frazzle. It works like this: the bells are set
for ten-minute periods and you go from class to class cov-

ering your child's daily schedule in about two hours. This is okay if you only have one child and you already *know* your school so you don't find yourself in the farthest bungalow looking for 209, which is on the second floor about two miles away. I frequently have at least three schedules to follow, and quite often the period is over before I decide whether to go to Billy's history class or Pat's biology or Ginger's geometry.

This year, though, I really thought I had it made. Bill was at home and we *planned*. He was to cover some of the classes and I would cover some—all decided in advance. Bill wanted to go to the classes where "somebody was having a little trouble," which seemed to be most of them. I didn't care. I just wanted to go to Ginger's English class because one day she brought home a paper with an A on it, and I wanted just one time to be the mama the teacher said "She's so smart" to. Usually *that* mama's either right in front of or right behind me, and I always want to slip out the side door before the teacher tells me that mine could do "so much better" if only he would *apply himself* or *get there on time* or *do her homework* or *pay attention*.

Anyway, as I said, this year we planned, and I did all right until third period. Then I got a little mixed up. Now that I think it over, it was just that I couldn't take it. Ginger's English class was more than I could ever hope for. Drunk with the praise from the teacher, I walked out of the room dazzled by the phrases ringing in my ears: "She's an extremely brilliant child . . . she has a real talent for writing . . . so well read . . . the most *superb* writer I have ever encountered in a sophomore class."

I floated right past wherever I was supposed to go and took a front seat in the French teacher's class. She was a charming, vivacious person—really *French*.

"*Bon jour, Bon jour,*" she chirruped, "you are . . . ?"

"Mrs. Rutland—Pat and Ginger's mother," I said proudly, still all aglow from Ginger's English.

"Oh, *non, non, non*—they come fifth period," she said.

"Well, I'll just wait," said I. And I did until suddenly it dawned on me that if I did not belong there I must belong somewhere else. I looked at my notes, and I was supposed to be in room 306 or was it 316?

Smiling apologetically I maneuvered myself past the interested parents and the now lecturing French teacher.

Room 316 was empty, so I went back up to 306, slipped quietly in, and took my seat. The teacher was lecturing on government. After class he smiled at me, "You are . . . ?"

"Mrs. Rutland—Pat and Ginger's mother." I beamed.

"But I don't have either of them."

"*Billy's* mother?" I said, hopefully.

He shook his head. "No, I don't have him either," he said sadly. Then, brightening, "I had Elsie two years ago."

It must have been 326 I was supposed to go to.

I went back to the French class—and took a seat.

"Non, non, non," she said. "Not yet, not yet. This is fourth period."

I went outside and saw Bill standing in the hall. He was methodically jotting notes such as "late three times last week . . . missing assignment one, page three; assignment four, page twenty-five."

"How're you doing?" he asked.

"Fine, fine!" I said, glancing at his schedule. This was my lunch, next period was French, and the next Pat's English and Ginger's biology.

The bell rang and Bill moved on. I went back to the French class.

"Now, now," said the French teacher as if complimenting a not very bright student who had just mastered a difficult problem. "*This* is the time. *You* are right."

Like I say, this was "know your school night," and after hearing the French teacher rattling off those French phrases I now know why Pat can only stare at her blankly and say "*Repetez—s'il vous plait.*"

One more class to go. I started out in Pat's English class. Then I remembered that Mr. Nuban was Ginger's biology teacher and I had never thanked him for trying so hard with Billy last year, so I decided to go there.

The tardy bell rang as I dashed down the hall, and the French teacher who was closing her door opened it again to say, "Are you lost *again*, Mrs. Rutland?"

Back home, Bill, checking his written notes, talked expertly and intelligently about paying attention in history and how many steps it was from gym to biology and who should not be late and physiology assignment three, page twenty, which was missing. All I could do was babble incoherently about what Ginger's English teacher said and how I got lost three times in the French class. Whereupon the twins began to wail about how could I be so stupid and how would they face the French teacher in the morning?

Parents—all of us, stupid or not—are organized. We are *running everything.* Which brings me to a point a friend of mine made in regard to the increase in juvenile delinquency. Perhaps, she said, *crime* is the only thing they can organize and run without adult interference.

I remember the day my ten-year-old son crawled into the car and cried his heart out. For the third straight Little League game he had sat on the bench. Oh, there were reasons: he had just moved up from the minors to the majors, he was untried, and the manager's son played shortstop too. If they were on a sandlot, my husband said, and the kids were running it, he'd get his chance.

And he would have. I remember when I was a kid and my brothers, to make two teams (a team consisted of maybe three or four players), would let me play, and I was permitted to bat with a plank to make things more equitable—until I got too good with the plank and the other team protested that I had to use the regular bat like everyone else. But everyone was playing and for fun.

Now they play for the championship, and a team is in first, second, or third place or it's in the gutter, and the teams overflow and half of the boys are sitting heartsick on the benches and the other half play their hearts out with their whole world watching on the sidelines, and when a boy strikes out it's all he can do not to pucker up and cry, and it's no longer just for fun.

Oh, there are grand moments. Like the time my son was the regular first baseman, and with the score three to two in favor of the other team and two men on base, he clobbered the ball straight over the fence for a home run and victory. He and his daddy came home sailing!

But I keep thinking of that other day and the other boys on the benches. And I keep thinking maybe the championship contests start too soon.

Maybe it's all too soon. Take now. One of my daughters is a senior Girl Scout. For the last two years she has been reading to a blind lady who translates into braille for blind children. She has now completed her hospital aide training and also works as a volunteer at the children's hospital. The girls in her troop are raising money and making plans for a trip to

Hawaii next year. But she and one other girl are all that's left of the original troop. The rest got bored with badges and meetings and "baby stuff" long before they reached this worthwhile stage.

And my son dropped out of Boy Scouts soon after I bought his equipment—as did several other boys of my acquaintance in different troops.

So, you say, what am I saying? I ought to reach some conclusion. Which brings me back to my original point. What can you do about it anyway?

Of course it's ten years too late. But I know what I would do if I could do it over again. Or maybe what I wouldn't do. I wouldn't be a Brownie leader or a den mother. I wouldn't take any youth leader training. I wouldn't care if my kids didn't join anything—unless maybe it was some organization with trained leaders in charge of crafts and sports (not bungling mamas like me). Only in this day and time these organizations are rather hard to find. Just this morning a mother, who thought she could escape the den mother bit by placing her son in the YMCA, showed me a block of wood delivered to her husband by a fellow member of his Indian Guides (a YMCA father and son group). The husband was to carve something out of the wood. "For instance," said the man, "my Indian name is 'Big Bear' so I carved a bear out of mine." I don't know what her husband said, but I know what mine would say.

Anyway, if I could do it over again, I wouldn't join anything. I'd just stay home and clean house and bake cookies and read books. I'd read books to the kids and with the kids and by myself. And I'd go over their lessons carefully each night with no interference from meetings or Little League or mothers' auxiliary meetings. They might not know how to screen paint or carve soap, but they would read and write better. And maybe we would make a skirt together or bake a cake or play Ping-Pong—or go out and do nothing.

But right now I've got to hurry—potato salad for my daughter's swimming party and potluck with the Girl Scouts, and we have a Little League game tonight. And for Pete's sake don't tell anyone I said this. They might put me off the PTA board.

Patty-Jo and Ginger as angels at Sacramento's Oak Park Congregational Church
Christmas pageant, Sacramento, 1954

6

You Have to Be Rich

A nother thing about being a mama is you have to be rich. Only it doesn't always work out that way. Regardless of the Rockefellers and Fords, it is true that the rich get richer and the poor get children.

I'm the children type myself. And it worries me a little that the only people I know who can afford four bathrooms don't have any children at all. What can you *do* with four bathrooms if you don't have three girls who constantly have to put their hair up in curlers and a boy who constantly has to brush the curls out? You just don't have the pressing need.

As I said to Bill, "Please, if we can't have the house, can we just have the four bathrooms?"

Not that four bathrooms are any guarantee of privacy. Years ago when the children were young I would retreat behind the locked door of the bathroom with my magazine.

Then would come the inevitable pounding on the door and/or the inevitable bloodcurdling scream, "Make Billy leave me alone!" Or "Where's my cap?" Or "How do you spell *cat?*" Or "Can I have a peanut butter and jelly sandwich?" Or in some rare instances, "Let me in *now*, I gotta *go*."

Anyway, now that the children are older and I have three bathrooms—they still pile up in mine. So I must say, it doesn't help. It's really *you* they want. But you don't know this at first, so you keep trying to accumulate things like bathrooms and televisions and hi-fis and encyclopedias and pianos, which you think are essential to their welfare. It's too late when you find out that nothing beats a library for research and nobody's going to play the piano anyway—and if they did, you couldn't afford lessons because there you are with *all those payments.*

Some payments are essential. With six in a family how can you live without a washing machine? And six people need at least six pairs of shoes—usually at the same time. That's another reason the rich get richer and the poor get poorer.

People without children can concentrate on making money. People with children have to concentrate on spending it—or stretching it.

My mama was a stretcher. "A woman," she would say, "can throw more out of the back door with a teaspoon than a man can bring in the front door with a shovel."

Consequently nothing went out our back door with or without a teaspoon. I was mortally afraid to throw out a crust of bread for fear "I would hunger for it some day." If the dog couldn't eat it—we did. Every scrap of leftover meat was ground up for hash or meat patties; leftover bread crusts came back to the table as luscious puddings topped with stewed prunes and heavenly meringue. Leftover rice became a pudding too—this time filled with plump juicy raisins. Believe me, you couldn't find a leftover spoonful to throw out.

Mama had an answer for the clothes problem too. I think she always regretted the fact that I was a girl and couldn't wear the pants that had already been handed down from Sam to Ed. But she made up for this freak of nature.

"My, that's beautiful," she would say, eyeing the dress of a more fortunate friend or relative. "When you finish with it, please give it to me for Eva Elsie." And they would. And Mama would take up, cut down, hem, and I would have a new dress. I think I wore hand-me-downs from everybody in town. Which proves that if you're not rich, you had better be clever.

Once I decided to be clever. I don't exactly know what prompted it unless it was the fact that I was broke. Formals were way out of range, and this special boy had asked Elsie to this special dance. And anyway, how would you feel if people kept saying, "All those girls and *you don't sew?*"

"Nothing to it," I told Elsie. The dance was three days away. How many times had I seen my mama whip up a formal in one afternoon—with a few yards of gingham from the five-and-ten?

One thing I forgot. I wasn't my mama. And Elsie wasn't me.

Any nineteen-cents-a-yard cotton would have suited me. For Elsie—nothing but the best, and cotton has gone up since my day.

It was just a simple dress with a tight bodice and a full skirt. "Tighter, Mama," Elsie kept saying, and I kept taking it up until it was so tight she couldn't get it on. So I had to go buy some more gold cotton for another bodice, which after two days I got almost tight enough and more or less onto the skirt. Elsie was a lot of help. She kept telling me it was "horrible" and couldn't I fix this or that?

When the young man arrived I was sewing madly on one side of the hem, Patty-Jo was sewing on the other, and Elsie

was searching through her closet for something else to wear.
Not being able to produce a suitable substitute, she put on my
more or less finished product, took one look at the sagging
waistline, and decided not to go. But it was an important date
for the young man—his graduation party—so I put my foot
down there. Finally Patty-Jo and I wrapped a piece of leftover
material around her waist like a cummerbund, which im-
proved the whole thing no end—made it almost presentable.
Elsie flounced unhappily off, and I collapsed in my cluttered
bedroom and vowed "never again."

Now I don't mean to imply that making hash and being
clever are the only ways to stretch. There are other ways like
buying out of season, buying in bulk, following the sales, and
shopping at the right store.

For me none of these plans have proved feasible.

Buying out of season: In the summer I am so busy buying
cottons and playsuits and swimsuits that I have to pass up
those smart winter coats and woolen skirts that "can now be
had for a mere fraction of the original cost." And in winter,
quite the other way. Besides, by next season, the children will
all be at least two feet taller.

Buying in bulk: It's all I can do to get tomorrow's ham-
burger, to say nothing of half a cow.

Following the sales: Always they come at my lowest financial ebb, or it's sheets when I need shoes or vice versa.

Shopping at the "right store": Now this is where I shine.
For me, the right store is the one that carries the copies of the
copies of the original, and plenty of them in all sizes. Well,
let's put it this way—this is where I did shine until the kids
became older and more discriminating. "Mother, let's not go
in that junky place." Or "*Everybody* will have one."

A friend of mine solved this by giving her child a lump sum each season and letting her shop for herself. But let's face it—lump sums are out of my category, and what we have must be spent for whatever item each child needs most.

So I long for the days when they were young and would follow where I led them—mostly into the five-and-ten.

I'll never forget one special Christmas in the five-and-ten.

The fat lady glared at me as I lunged across her, upsetting her packages. But I had to rescue that rocket gun from Billy. It was worth more than the combined wealth of all five of us.

With this mission accomplished, I turned to apologize, but Elsie blocked the way. "Mama, what must I do?" she whispered frantically, "Billy bought Ginger the same thing I bought her!"

I was picking up the lady's packages, but by that time Patty-Jo had trod on her toes and the apology was futile. Her glance told me clearly what I already knew—the basement of the five-and-ten three days before Christmas was no place to bring four children.

It was all on account of Bill and the measles and the Christmas spirit, and right then I wished I hadn't heard of any of them.

Humbug, I thought, remembering Bill's lamentations about the commercialization of Christmas.

"Christmas is for the children," he had said. "A few toys for them this year and . . ."

But I didn't agree. Christmas, I thought, is for everybody. And Christ is there—yes, even in the commercial practice of giving.

Those things you get—that box of cookies from far-away Aunt Emma, whose sight is failing and whose cash is low. The spicy odor of sugar and cinnamon takes you back to the warmth and security of that spotless kitchen where a young and vigorous Aunt Emma mixed cookie dough. The warm robes from your parents for the children, and the watch for which you secretly yearned—it's there with a card from your husband, a gift that represents spare cash carefully tucked away and maybe a few lunchless days. His love envelops you as the watch encircles your wrist. You feel loved and wanted. Your cup runneth over.

The getting, the giving, the remembering, and the loving. They're all part of the Christmas spirit. And if Christmas is for everybody, it's for the children too. And it's all for them— the giving as well as the getting—or so I argued.

Anyway, it was in this spirit that I decided to let the children buy the presents that they would give—really buy them—not just go with me to select them. Now in some families this would be easy—they could just save a little from their regular allowances. But in mine—well, let's face it— there's hardly enough loose change floating around for anyone to count on that promised allowance.

But this year would be different. I determined I would set up a system of jobs whereby the children could really earn their money for Christmas (you know—twenty-five cents for window washing, fifteen cents for dusting, etc.). Just two rules—no goldbricking on work, no welching on pay (unlike the promised allowances).

The measles threw the whole project off, cutting down on the twins' earning capacity and on my time. That explains why on earth I had all four of them shopping at one time. And besides buying gifts, we had to visit Santa and buy two pairs of shoes.

Bright and early this Tuesday morning before Christmas, I paid off—payroll ranging from $2.15 to $1.35. I stifled the impulse to tell them just to get some trinket for each other, that we could buy Daddy's gift together and vice versa with my own. In answer to queries about my needs, I said handkerchief, ashtray. Anyway, they seemed quite proud and satisfied with their wages—no complaints, no comparisons, each had what he or she had earned.

With such wealth, where could we go but to the five-and-ten? And that's where I deposited ten-year-old Elsie and six-year-old Ginger, with instructions to shop and meet me at the cosmetics counter. I felt a few misgivings, but they seemed confident. They had more faith in the capacity of a dollar than I had.

Billy and the other twin I took with me to the post office. The packages for home were just getting off—the measles again. I finally got them mailed with only two distractions—a minor squabble over a discarded comic book and a skating exhibition by Billy from one end of the post office to the other. Eventually we hurried back to the five-and-ten.

Elsie and Ginger were complacently waiting. They had bought everybody's gift but each other's—and had money left over! What did they buy, I wondered, looking at the curious and odd-shaped packages. But I took heart. This wouldn't be so bad. I decided to see Santa Claus and get the shoes, and then return to the five-and-ten.

That was a mistake. We had to stand in line for an hour to see Santa Claus. He was quite a vociferous Santa—but understanding: "Now, now, girls, let me talk to the boys first. You know boys can't stand still like girls. They wiggle and twist and pull on things." And I breathed a sigh of relief as

Billy released his hold on the overhanging decorations and moved forward. After expressing our heartfelt desires (he was a well-trained Santa—he didn't definitely promise anything), and laden with his gifts of candy canes and three-dimensional comic books, we moved on to the shoe department. Then, after a hasty lunch, my horde and I, and my aching feet, went back to the five-and-ten.

I told Elsie to take care of Ginger, while I concentrated on Pat and Billy. God bless the five-and-ten, I thought, as they made their purchases quickly and carefully, and within range of their pocketbooks. Things were going well. I switched charges with Elsie. She could help Pat and Billy buy my gifts while I helped Ginger select Elsie's. Ginger bought coloring books and crayons for Elsie and insisted on one for herself.

"You might need the money," I cautioned. But she insisted, so I acquiesced. After all, it was her money; she earned it.

Billy lumbered near. "Mama," he whispered, "I'm going to get these slate sets for the twins. They're only nineteen cents.

"But you have their gifts."

"Well, I'm going to give them two gifts," he announced. "I still have some money. Oh, and Mama, wouldn't Elsie just love this bracelet?" Yes, she would, and I love you, I thought. I had often wondered if he would be as generous with his own possessions as he was with my apples and oranges when the gang came around. Now I know, I thought, as he recklessly spent every penny.

I was really proud. They were so carefully picking the things they knew the recipient would want—too carefully, in fact.

For it was then that Elsie whispered frantically that she and Billy had selected the same things for the twins.

"It's all right," I whispered back, "Billy bought them two things." And Patty-Jo crawled over the fat lady's toes to me.

"Mama," she said, "Ginger's crying."

That was an understatement. Ginger was alarming the whole store. She made her way toward me screaming, the tears falling like rain down her cheeks.

"Ginger, what . . . ?"

"I didn't get Daddy anything."

"Oh, all right. Ssssh! We'll get him something."

"But I bought myself something!"

"Sh! Sssssh! That's all right. We'll get Daddy something."

"But *I spent all my money!*"

"Sh! Sssssh!" Everybody's attention was centered on us.

"*I don't want this old coloring book. Take it back!*"

"Ssssssssh! Ssssssssh! I'll give you some money to buy . . ."

"Take it back. *I wanta buy Daddy something!*"

"Sssssh!" The fat lady gave me a "how can you be so mean—surely you can afford a quarter for her daddy" look.

"Ginger, I'll give you . . . sssh! Look, I'll lend it to you—you can vacuum the floors tomorrow!"

"*I don't want this old book. Take it back. I wanta buy Daddy something!*"

I appealed to a salesgirl.

"Look, would you exchange this coloring book for this . . . this"—I looked around— "this clothes brush? My little girl bought it for herself and now she's spent all her money and she didn't get her daddy anything and . . ." I felt rather silly. The store was crowded, and it was only a nineteen-cent coloring book.

But the clerk understood.

"Oh, is that why she was crying?" It involved calling the floorwalker and a dime furtively passed from me to the sales-girl (the clothes brush was twenty-nine cents). But it was worth it. The uproar ceased, the tear-stained face smiled, and a little girl happily clutched a clothes brush in her pudgy hand, with not even a backward glance at the once coveted coloring book. Never was a gift so truly given.

Even the fat lady smiled as we left the store.

Never did a few earned dollars give so much pleasure—the secretive smiles and the whispers back and forth, "Oh, Ginger, you'll just love what I bought you!" "Elsie, I bought Billy . . ." "Sssh, he'll hear you." "Oh, Pat, I just can't wait—you'll just love what I bought you."

Everybody on the bus smiled as they listened to their chatter. I marveled that the visit to Santa was completely forgotten.

And at home—the hiding of the gifts, the furtive wrap-ping of the packages, placing them under the Christmas tree.

One thing bothered me. What about Christmas morn-ing? Would the little gifts selected with such love and care be ignored and lost among the big things—the cowboy suit, the cradles and dolls?

I was oh so careful Christmas morning to make a big display over mine—a red wreath and Christmas bell for my coat lapel, a bottle of perfume encased in a toy telephone, two barrettes for my hair, a handkerchief. How loudly I loved them all.

But I needn't have worried.

Billy was as grateful for the forty-two cent pop gun from Elsie as he was for the $9.95 gun and holster set. And there were as many expressions from the others: "Oh, Patty-Jo, thank you." "Oh, Billy, you knew I would want this, didn't you?"

My doubts were really dispelled when Ginger came to me carefully holding the necklace from Patty-Jo. "Mama, will you please keep this in your jewelry box for me?" And when Elsie wore the bracelet constantly for two whole weeks—the one Billy knew she would love. And when Daddy said (quite truthfully) that the clothes brush from Ginger was the most useful and needed gift in the house.

And there was the other thing.

There was Billy, two days after Christmas, standing before me and saying, "Santa Claus didn't really brings us those presents. You and Daddy bought them."

I started to protest. But I looked at Billy and he was smiling and the smile seemed to say, "I know. I know how lovingly and with what care you chose the cowboy suit and the football. I even know how it was about the bike you didn't buy. I know because I went shopping too."

And then I smiled back. For these were not the disillusioned eyes of a little boy saying good-bye to Santa Claus. These were the eyes of a little boy saying hello to the giving, the getting, the thoughtfulness, the pure loving kindness of Christmas—the eyes of a little boy who had really shared.

And I said then, God bless the five-and-ten.

It was a real wrench for me to pass up the five-and-ten when the pickets were there. You know the brave young people that decided segregation was wrong anywhere—schools, bus stations, lunch counters—and picketed all over the country.

But pass it up I did. This was bigger than my pocketbook. These young people were bigger than me—and I could not let them down.

Patty-Jo and Ginger on pony, Sacramento, 1954

7

You Have to Be Smart

There's this other thing about being a mama: you have to be smart. Actually, when you come right down to it, this is most important.

The point is that in this capitalistic, machine-taking-over society, if you're going to exist at all, you have to know how to do something—and not just how to dig ditches, as I keep telling Billy. The machines do that. So it's the fundamentals that count, like "what are you going to be when you grow up?" And yes, I know all about those "mother don't dominate—let him follow his own bent" admonitions. But, believe me, some mama and papa direction is necessary, else they'd all turn out to be firemen or movie stars.

I remember a dearly loved but proud uncle who was a doctor in a little country town in Georgia. (He intended to make his "start" there, but that was fifty years ago and he's still there. He has his own office building, owns half the town, serves and is adored by white and colored patients—and that's pretty successful for a Negro doctor in a country town in Georgia.)

Anyway, said one of this uncle's five children to my mother one day, "Aunt Eva, do you know what I'm gonna be when I grow up?"

"No, George," said Mama, "What are you going to be?"

George expanded his chest and announced proudly, "I'm gonna be a pigpen fixer!"

"Fred, you'd better bring those children out of the country," said my mama.

But Uncle Fred was not to be outdone.

"Owen," he said, "what are you going to be?"

"I'm gonna be a rich man. You thought I was gonna be a doctor, didn't you?" chuckled Owen.

You know something? He is a rich man. Well, he's a banker and all of them are rich, aren't they?

But it doesn't always turn out that way. Most pigpen fixers have changed their minds by the time they are grown, and there they are not knowing how to do anything but fix pigpens.

And that's where mamas and papas come in.

By some devious means you have to slip in a little preparation to be something else when the pigpen fixing palls. And it's hard to be devious about reading and writing, or to convince a certain first baseman that algebra is more important than baseball when Willie Mays just signed for $110,000. As a matter of fact, I begin to have doubts myself. Now, if Billy was as good a bat man as he is a glove man.

Anyway, that's not my department. Algebra is. And I proudly quote one of the children's classmates: "Let's go over to your house to study algebra cause *your mom is a whizz!*" I ought to be. I've had four years of it—all the way from junior high to college.

Algebra is one thing I am better at than Bill. Trouble is—he *thinks*. And no matter if he does get the answers quicker than I do, I keep telling him you're not supposed to think it out—you're supposed to work it out with Xs and Ys. And that's not easy because of the "changing methods of education." Remember when we went to school how simple it was? You put all the Xs and Ys on one side and the numbers on another, and if you changed sides you changed signs, and you went on from there. Now you do something called "inverse operation," which means elimination by subtraction, and it all comes out the same—only getting there is more complicated.

But that's nothing when you consider the idiotic problems like the one Billy and I struggled with the other night. "Two bicycle riders, A and B, start at the same time, 3:00 p.m., riding toward each other from points 20 miles apart. A rides 15 miles per hour and B rides 10 miles per hour. Where and at what time will they meet?"

Now doesn't that give you a sort of "who cares" feeling? You really have to take the long view, and I must say we found it rather difficult when Billy's calculations were more of the batting-average type and mine more of the "how much change from a dollar for one loaf of bread and three pounds of apples" type. (At today's prices that's no change at all.)

You know what I think about education? I think we could do with less *progress* because you still read and write and figure the same old-fashioned way.

For example, take reading. After you were taught to sound out "cat," "dog," and "hen," you found everything else pretty darn com-pre-hen-si-ble. And that's better than monkey being monkey because it has a tail on the Y. Even Webster couldn't remember all those words from pictures, and the Egyptians gave up hieroglyphics thousands of years ago.

Not being able to read is dangerous, especially in California, where, if you are not careful, you get categorized right out of school without even knowing it. They call it the XYZ program, wherein all pupils in high school are placed in three categories—X (above average), Y (average), or Z (below average).

Now on the surface this looks pretty good—you know, "slow" learners separated from "fast." Only in California everything has to be way, way out. Why, they have this system so mixed up you don't know an A from a D. If you are an X and you get an A it is really an A, and if you get a B it's really an A. But if you are a Y and you get an A in the *same* class, it is an A; if you get a B, it is a B. Almost as if you're getting paid for being "brainier" even if you do the same as someone less brainy. Now if you are a Z, don't worry about what your As and Bs mean because with the milk toast curriculum you are fed, you'll never get into college anyway. The Zs never even get exposed to the higher math, language, and college prep courses.

But they finish. High school graduates going nowhere— pigpen fixers with an embossed diploma.

All right, so their egos are preserved. So some of us are destined to be pigpen fixers, and this gives us dignity. I'd prefer a more honest out. Let them learn a trade and four precious years won't be wasted.

Only it is not the pigpen fixers that bother me. It's the highly normal, slightly lazy Negro children like mine who just might slip into the wrong category. And if you think I have a chip on my shoulder, you are quite right.

I recall a child of a certain leading citizen. She had been observed and tested in elementary school and placed with an accelerated group—children in the genius category who had been given extra work, new and varied experiences. She had covered two years of schoolwork in one and was passed to junior high. In junior high for some reason unfathomable to her parents, she was unhappy at school and lost interest in her work. Now this child's father happened to attend a social function that one of this child's teachers also attended. In the conversation, this teacher mentioned that he wished the child was in one of his other groups. In this way, the father made the startling discovery that his bright child had been placed with the slow learners in this particular class. As a result the mother made a visit to the school, asked to see the child's records, and learned that such was the case in all of the child's classes. The startled counselor, observing the elementary school transcript (stamped "Accelerated" in big red letters) could offer no logical explanation.

It does seem a strange coincidence that this child happened to be colored, and the majority of the children in the Z group in this particular school also happened to be colored.

And I recall the case of a certain Japanese gardener who appealed to one of his Caucasian customers about his son. His son had maintained a straight A average throughout junior high, was planning to attend the university, and needed and deserved an X status. But he was placed as a Y. My friend, his customer, advised him to see the principal of the school. He took off from his work, dressed carefully, and went to the school, where for a whole day he was shunted from one office to another. After he persisted, he was finally allowed the change in status. The boy graduated with honors, is now attending the university, and is doing well.

These two cases of course were quickly and positively resolved. But I cannot help but wonder about the many minority children whose fathers do not happen to meet their children's teachers socially or whose parents may not even be aware of XYZ ratings or college credits or how to cope with this particular problem.

And anyway, why am I worrying about the "don't know what it's all about and wouldn't know what to do about it if they did" parents when here we are, fairly intelligent, pretty well-educated parents, and we don't know what to do about it either. Oh, we can raise Cain and be sure they're in the right class and right category and all that; and we can talk until our heads fall off, but that won't always make Junior produce if Junior doesn't want to.

Once we became so overwhelmed by the "Mama-Papa responsibility for Junior's education when Junior doesn't care a whit about it" problem that we went to one of those family counselors, which is something that nowadays, if you are a really conscientious parent, you sooner or later feel you must do.

The counselor turned on me. Why, why, did I feel this tremendous anxiety? This was something between Junior and the school. Surely the school was big enough.

Not wanting to further expose my guilty anxieties, I kept my mouth shut and wouldn't say what I really thought—which was that way down deep the school just didn't care as much as I did.

Which brings me to the counseling program. Just as youngsters can get categorized out of school, so they can get counseled out of careers. According to one counselor, speaking to our teenage group and lamenting the fact, we seem to be adopting England's class system in counseling: "Can the son of this poor laborer really find happiness as a doctor?" "Should I really advise this artistic Negro boy with definite skills in mechanical drawing to become an architect when the field for

Negroes is so limited?" "Should this boy with the limited vocabulary be encouraged in his ambitions to be a lawyer?"

Oh, the counselor may be sincere, but, I repeat, he does
not always care as I do. I don't really believe that Johnny will
be happier as a pigpen fixer just because his father is one or
that a really good Negro architect cannot open the door a little more or that a really ambitious boy can't improve his vocabulary if steered to the right courses.

Or maybe the counselor cannot "relate." I attended a session with a man who was writing a book on counseling minorities. He cited the case of a dedicated counselor who
visited the home of one of his Mexican pupils. While there,
the father brought home a pie. The family, one and all, gathered in a circle on the floor and delved into the pie with their
fingers. How then, asked this man in evident sincerity, could
this fastidious counselor relate to this boy?

What has pie eating got to do with biology? I wanted to
ask. What more could the visit indicate other than that a
quiet supervised study period might be helpful in the boy's
schedule? But I said nothing, for what I really wanted to say
was, why a book on counseling minorities anyway? You counsel them just like you counsel everyone else. Obviously, all
Mexican families do not eat with their fingers in the same
pot, as all white families do not eat on immaculate linen table-
cloths with highly polished silver!

Let us stick to the essentials, I wanted to say. How capable are the children, how ambitious—and how best to plot the
course and pave the way to whatever they want to be?

But maybe it's not the school or the counselor. Maybe
it's me. Me with my very average, slightly lazy children, me
and my minority status, me and my black skin. Maybe I'm
sensitive.

Maybe nothing. You're darn right. I am sensitive.

Who has not asked, "Who am I? Whence did I come?" Many Americans can answer with pride, "My forefathers came over on the Mayflower." "I can trace my ancestry to a castle in Scotland, to a nobleman of France, to an English peer." It is true that some could be traced to a debtor's prison or an equal disgrace. But that shame has long been obliterated, buried, lost in the vast majority of white faces, leveled off in the leveling sea of American democracy.

But I have a trademark that shouts to the world that my ancestors came over in the belly of a slave ship. My roots go no further—from royal African tribe or scum, I know not. My ancestry beyond the slave ship is lost as surely as that of my white friends from the debtor's prison. But the mark of the slave ship is not. By the color of my skin ye shall know my shame.

It is not an easy thing to grow up in a world that has placed a stamp of shame upon your heritage. No matter that the shame is not your own. No matter that you were only a pawn in another's greed for wealth and power. Somehow you bow to that other man's philosophy. The shame transmits itself to you, and you lower your head when confronted with the symbols of your past—a bandanaed Aunt Jemima, a black-faced comedian with a Negro dialect, a bare-footed boy with his face sunk in a watermelon.

And the shame becomes a burden on your heart, a chip on your shoulder, carried with you into the marketplaces, the streets, the schools.

And if you are a Negro child in an "integrated" school, you don't exactly understand why the chip is there and you don't know what to do about it. You put your head on your desk when they talk about slavery, and the other kids snicker and look at you. Or you sock a guy who calls you "nigger." But the hurt doesn't go away.

And if you are the mother of a Negro child in an "integrated" school, you may know vaguely why the chip is there, but even you are not really sure why, and even you don't know what to do about it or even how to distinguish between the chip and fact—whether your child really belongs in the Z category or whether the counselor is prejudiced; whether they really don't have an opening in the Scout troop or whether they don't want your child; whether the part of the maid is really the only role she can take in the class play.

And the chip can lead you astray.

For instance, in a nearby city a very bright boy had written a musical based on one of Mark Twain's classics, entered it in competition with several others, and emerged the winner. The prize was the production of the play by the students. Everything was going fine until several Negro parents learned that their children were to portray slaves and wasn't that a shame! Children were snatched out of the play, protests rose against its production, the NAACP was called in, and the newspapers had a ball. The poor student who adapted the play (I understand that he happened to be a Negro) had to consult a psychiatrist. The uproar made him feel he had betrayed his people—and there he was torn between shame and his pride in the folklore and spirituals that had made him choose this particular book. At one point it was doubtful that the play would be produced, and when it finally was, the patrons had to step across the NAACP picket line.

Personally, I'm glad the production played to a full house and I am everlastingly sorry that I didn't go.

Because there it was again—the chip and the shame. The sophisticated Negro leaders deny this. It's not what we think, they say—it's what *they* think. And their position is somewhat vindicated by people who contended, among other derogatory remarks, that Negroes wouldn't be portrayed as clowns if they didn't act like clowns.

To these people I would like to say, "*Slaves* were not *clowns.*" And to the shamed leaders, "What *they* think is not nearly so important as what *we* think."

Because I grew up in a southern town and was educated in a segregated school where Negro history was a required part of the curriculum and where you learned about Crispus Attucks and Booker T. as well as George Washington; because of my father and Paul Lawrence Dunbar, I think I escaped the shame altogether, and the chip rests lightly on my shoulder.

Paul L. Dunbar was a singer of songs, a teller of tales, a weaver of tears and laughter. It was the laughter that attracted me. I laughed with him long and heartily, for I was very young then and did not know that I laughed at myself. Later I was grateful for this ten-carat, gold-plated gift—that ability to laugh at oneself. And grateful for more—that through him I found my roots.

It was my father, who loved to read, who first introduced me to Dunbar. I can see him now as he read from the big black volume containing *The Life and Works of Paul Lawrence Dunbar,* standing tall and slender and departing from his customary cultured accents to simulate the dialect of the early Negro mammy who, though she extoled that "evah mawnin' on this place, seem lak I mus' lose my grace," never did. And the Negro father who loved his "Little brown baby wif' sparklin' eyes"; and the Negro preacher who taught "de Lawd's intention, evah sence de worl' began, was dat His almighty freedom Should belong to *evah* man" but cautioned his followers, "Don't run an tell yo' mastahs dat I's preachin' discontent." Through this medium I learned to love and respect my people. I learned of the Negro soldier's bravery, the preacher's diplomacy, Malindy's singing. I learned of a heritage rich with love and loyalty, a black man with a faith and patience so great that it can only be compared to that of the biblical Job, a man of humility and compassion, who laughed and loved through a period of despair, who emerged triumphant with no hate in his soul, a man to be proud of.

I tried to pass this heritage on to my children.

I remember a day when Elsie was to give a pantomime in her dramatics class. I suggested "Encouragement," a poem about a coquettish Negro lass of slavery time who coaxes "Ike" to pop the question, a delightful strain that lends itself beautifully to pantomime. My children have always heard and enjoyed Dunbar's poetry, and this was a particular favorite. But reading and laughing about ourselves in the confines of our own living room was quite different from displaying this bit of our past before an audience of white classmates. I'll say this for Elsie—she tried. She mastered the difficult dialect, learned the poem, did a beautiful pantomime job. But at the last minute she balked, she could not quite bring herself to do it. "Don't urge her," cautioned my husband, "she isn't ready yet." And I had my own apprehensions, that old bugaboo of being stereotyped. Perhaps so, I said. Let it pass. She selected another pantomime, one without a racial taint.

But there came a day when she had to present a poem in English class—a last-minute search for a short one. Ah! Paul Lawrence Dunbar. I remembered an especially good short one, "Life." Good—it was nondialect and would do.

She learned and presented it, routinely naming the author. The teacher, bless her heart, was familiar with the name and fame of Paul Lawrence Dunbar and praised him to the class. Encouraged and proud, my daughter timidly offered, "I know some of his dialect poems."

"Wonderful," said the teacher. Would she share them with the class?

And out at last came the delightful "speak up, Ike, and 'spress yourself."

The class was enchanted. Would she do them for the other English classes? asked the teacher. Of course.

"And Mama," she said later, "do you know Timmy (a Negro boy) looked at me so funny—as if he were *ashamed!* Wasn't that silly?"

I smiled, remembering how recent was her own emancipation.

And was she stereotyped by this incident? Far from it. It was remembered only that she read well. The English teacher recommended her, and she was chosen to do the narration for the Christmas play, a coveted part. By binding her to her heritage, I had set her free.

There is more. This year she is in college, where teachers speak more freely, expressing their own opinions. One professor openly talked of the "backward southern Negro"—in fact, stated that there were no progressive Negroes in the South. Backed by pride in her heritage and bolstered by the knowledge of the many outstanding Negroes she had met in the South, timid little Elsie challenged this statement and aptly proved her point.

And, instead of being crushed by his remarks, as she would have been at one time, her only reaction was, "Gee, Mama, how can so-called *intelligent* people be so stupid?"

Pride had replaced the shame, and the chip was gone.

When I read of the sit-in strikes, the freedom riders, the marching voters, I think: they walk with pride, with the knowledge that into the Stars and Stripes are tightly woven the threads of the black man's love, his compassion, his patience, humility, bravery. And I think that democracy marches with them.

It is with the same kind of pride that we will overcome the subtle prejudices that lurk in our "integrated" schools. Our state school board is now campaigning to present a better image of the Negro in our textbooks. (The Negro is presenting a pretty good image of himself, incidentally—in both our junior colleges this year a Negro girl was chosen as homecoming queen.) Through FEPC (Fair Employment Practices Committee), more Negro teachers are being hired. Negro sororities and fraternities are conducting career conferences to supplement the guidance programs in our schools. One fraternity made the services of its members available to any student needing help with his studies. The conferences were attended by white as well as black youngsters. And more white than colored solicited help from the fraternity. True to our unspoken code of "total integration," not one youngster who asked was refused.

And somehow, with the giving we get. We project ourselves into the total picture. Someday we may become so much a part of it that we can don a bandana and sing a spiritual with no prejudice and much pride.

Elsie and Billy, Sacramento, 1959

8
Boy Meets Girl– But How?

I hate to keep saying this, and I certainly wouldn't want it breathed in the higher echelons of the NAACP, but another problem with being a mama today is integration. And don't misunderstand me. I'm all for integration, but it does have its problems.

One of its biggest problems is sex.

Now, if you are a mama, sooner or later sex is something you have to face. By sex I don't mean the "you must tell them about the birds and bees and the things that a nice girl doesn't do" routine. Although this routine is important. At least it is according to a doctor friend of mine who has been quite overwhelmed by the wailing "how did I get into this and why didn't somebody tell me" teenagers who visit his office. He blames the mamas.

So I try to inform and fortify mine.

You know those cozy little mother and daughter chats.

"What shall I wear?"

"The green . . ."

"Ooh, *that* old thing? It's horrible!"

"The blue . . ."

"Mama! We're just going to the show!"

"This . . ."

"Oh, that's horrible! And look at my skin. It's horrible, and my hair—ooh, what am I going to do?"

I accept this interest in her appearance as part of her growing up and I understand. Understand? I'm downright grateful.

When the children were younger their attention was all focused on me.

"Mama, when you bring the treats to school today, will you please wear that skinny red dress with no back and your glass slippers?"

That's because when you're a mama you have to be beautiful. And I don't mean that deep quiet beauty that shines from within. I mean the more obvious earthy beauty that prompts a child to say proudly, like Patty-Jo did in her five-year-old's fractured English, "Now, aren't you glad you wore your tight skirt and red high heels? See how all the mens whistles at you?"

These compliments are few and far between—the kind of thing a mama likes to preserve. How I wish I could frame that golden day Billy came home from kindergarten and chortled, "Gosh, Mama, you should see Andy's mama. She's gorgeous, she's beautiful, she's . . ." He searched for a more descriptive word. "Gosh, Mom, she's almost as pretty as *you*."

Mostly the comments are of the type Elsie made when I went to pick her up from the Fourth of July parade. Very pretty she looked too, in her red dress with her ponytail dangling. She was seated on one side of the NAACP float and a white girl was on the other side—depicting love and unity, black and white, or something. The sun was hot. I knew she was tired. I rushed to the appointed place—glad to be there early.

Was she grateful?

"Mama," she scolded on the way home, "why did you come so early? That girl's mama was telling her how pretty you were, and then you had to come and *let her see you!*"

I have even been introduced with a belligerent sigh. "Well, I know she's not very pretty but she's my mama just the same." And it does get to be strenuous.

"Mama, please don't clean house in those old blue jeans. Put on your black dress. Somebody might come by!"

So I'm not exactly sorry when Billy struggles to slick the curls out of his hair and Elsie decides she's horrible. At least I'm off the hook.

"Darling," I say, "I don't think you look too bad."

"Just look at my hair. Mama, can't I have it done? It's . . ."

"I know, *horrible!* But he must have liked something about you. He did ask you."

"Mama, just look at this . . . what am I going to wear?"

In this spirit of togetherness I try to broach the delicate subject. "You know, I think we should talk about other things."

"Oh, yes, Mama. I want you to tell me what to *do.*"

"Well," I say, glad she is going to be cooperative, "you know a girl always sets the pace. You must always remember to act like a lady. Quite often when passions get out of hand . . ."

"Oh, Mama, gosh—you want to tell me about kissing and petting and all that stuff. I just want to know what to talk about."

Somewhat diverted, I mention football, school, current events, none of which reassure her.

"I wish I was like Anne. *All* the boys like her."

"What does she talk about?"

"Mostly she just giggles."

"Well, giggle," I say. And that ends my sex instruction for the day.

Anyway, the sex problem that really makes me worry is the "how does boy meet girl and who's gonna take me to the dance?" problem, Also, *what* dance?

Now if you're white, this is relatively simple. (Well, as simple as anything ever could be for an adolescent.) It's the school dance or the frat dance, and it's the boy who sits next to you in chemistry.

Being colored, you've got problems. If it's the school dance, you just might be the only "member" there (integration, you know). And if it's a frat dance, don't worry—you won't be there. And the only colored boy you ever see is the one in your Spanish class and he's a real drip.

This is slightly exaggerated, but I just want to point out that the choice is limited. Because you have reached the sex-conscious stage.

I remember the little blue-eyed blonde who used to accompany Billy home when he was in kindergarten.

"Tan Billy tum over?" she would chant. "My drammama don't tare."

After the fourth day, weary of her persuasions, I did let Billy "tum over." Half an hour later, realizing I didn't know where "drammama" lived, I went frantically searching for him and found him complacently munching milk and cookies supplied by "dram-mama," who really didn't "tare."

And there was a little Jewish girl whom Billy followed home. This I heard from a friend of her mother's. For I was totally unaware of the visit.

Sally's mother had said, "She had talked and talked about this Billy Rutland, and when she finally brought him home I was amazed. For there had been nothing in her conversation to indicate that Billy was colored. He was the most beautiful child I had ever seen, and I was so glad that Sally was so unconscious of race or color that it had not occurred to her to mention it."

That was at six.

But suppose Sally should bring Billy home at sixteen.

Heaven forbid, the same mother would shriek. Because at six it is wonderful for Sally to be innocent and open-minded and democratic about race and such, but at sixteen the possibility exists that she might marry the boy, for heaven's sake.

And it isn't always the boy that they'll object to.

Take the case of the frantic Caucasian businessman who protested against his daughter's engagement to a Negro law student.

"Tim is perfect," he confessed to a friend, "all I could want in a son-in-law—courteous, kind, ambitious, intelligent. I find not one single thing against him except that he is colored. But what would my friends say? It might hurt my business."

And the very dear Caucasian friend who confided to me: "You know, I was surprised in a discussion with friends the other day to hear my husband say that he would have absolutely no objection to his child marrying a Negro. This was something we had never discussed privately. But I was glad, for I felt the same way. *After all, they could always go to France to live.*"

For her mother's heart cried out against the pressures that her son would experience married to a Negro in America.

And my mother's heart understood. What mother would deliberately throw her son into a lion's den?

So I don't really blame Sally's mama.

But it sure complicates things for me and mine, that sharp dividing line between six and sixteen.

You go complacently along being a good Scout or Blue-bird or what have you. Then all of a sudden—wham! You're out. Even in the organizations you are already in.

Like the time Elsie was appointed chairman of the dance committee of her Girl Scout troop and she and I both wondered why—this being no ordinary dance. The Royal Order of Eagle Scouts, or whatever they're called, was having its conclave and recruiting girls from the various troops to be guests at the grand ball.

"Since I'm chairman, I'll have to go," grimaced Elsie, turning from the phone by which she was arranging girls, chaperones, and transportation. "So will you chaperone? Then I can sit with you and I won't be alone."

She didn't expect anything.

Certainly not what she got.

I don't know what the other girls expected.

Of course the handsome young men in full dress and full decoration—their banners and medals proclaiming each of them a proud member of the Royal Order of Eagle Scouts. This we had expected. But not a selected escort for each girl. Not a beautiful corsage. Each girl was swept gaily away on the arm of her escort.

And for Elsie too—the corsage, the escort. A fine young gentleman—a little younger than Elsie—neat, clean, full dress. But the absence of banners and medals placed him apart—identified him as not of the Royal Order. His brown face proclaimed that he was there for one purpose—to serve as Elsie's escort.

I sat with the mothers on the side and watched Elsie chatting with her young man, watched them take a turn about the floor, return and sit alone, watched them both smiling desperately—in and yet *out*. Remembered Elsie's "I can sit with you." She was even denied that dignity.

My eyes circled the floor—one other young man not in uniform. Chinese and dancing with a Chinese girl.

"Yes, lovely girls—beautiful music." I spoke mechanically, my heart across the floor with Elsie.

"I was so embarrassed," she said to me much later when we were at home alone. "Why didn't they just tell me not to come?"

I recognized her embarrassment not as an indictment of her escort but rather of the fact that he did not belong and was chosen—no, recruited—because she was what she was.

It was then that I lashed out at Sally's mother. No matter which mama had perpetrated this incident, no matter that it could have been kindness—*somebody has to escort that nice colored girl.*

"Don't let these people embarrass you," I said. "These are the conformists—the little people. Banding together in their cliques, their societies—afraid to deviate. You will meet bigger people, so secure themselves that they can look beyond color—and cash. These will be the people worth knowing."

In my heart I apologized to Sally's mama. I do know how she feels.

But I'm Elsie's mama and Billy's and the twins'. And it's their pride I must preserve, *their* happiness.

It wasn't long after this that Elsie dropped out of the Girl Scouts. I was sorry. She enjoyed reading to the blind lady, and the hospital work was good training for her. But I understood.

Anyway, as I say, the part of sex that bothers me is the how does boy meet girl?

Any mother knows that dancing and dating is part of growing up. That's why I joined—in fact, was a charter member of—the Sacramento Chapter of Jack & Jill (J & J).

Now our charter says our purpose is "to provide a constructive, educational, recreational, social, and cultural program for the children; and by this medium of contact create a greater bond of friendships for the children and their parents or guardians." But what it really means is that we Negroes are so scattered (integration, you know)—and well, you know how it is when they reach high school, so let's see that our kids get together somehow.

Only this proved to be more complicated than the PTA, because this too is a mama-run national organization that requires a whole raft of planners, programmers, financial secretaries, and the like, to take care of the mechanical details and endless installations, teas, et cetera, that accompany any mama-run organization—not to mention the group sponsors and chaperones who have to be on hand for the educational and cultural activities of the children such as snow trips, dancing, roller-skating, and horseback riding. This is all right but it does get expensive, even at the group rate. The horseback riding was $2 *per* child *per* lesson. The culture I am looking for could be had for a few rock 'n roll records and punch and cookies.

Only to be told (and who's kidding whom?) that this is not a social organization, we should stress the finer things, and why don't we take the group to the symphony concert? Nothing against symphonies, you understand, only you don't have to join a club to go. One bright spot though—we had a teenage conference that was a humdinger. Sprinkled among the dances and hayrides were wonderful career workshops.

The theme was "new horizons," and we had excellent consultants including an architect, an engineer, professors from the nearby state college, and a state senator.

The state senator did run into a little snag, and I can't report it accurately because I wasn't there. I did linger at the door of this workshop and debate about whether to sit in, but decided out of loyalty that I should attend my husband's workshop on the space age.

I don't know what happened at the senator's workshop, but it seems they had a hot session going, so hot, in fact, that the senator stormed out in the middle of it never to return. Seems it developed into a battle of wits between him and the teenagers, and with no other adult in there to tone them down. Poor guy. One thing about Negro teenagers of today—there are no holds barred.

From what we could gather from the teenagers, they took issue with his bright version of new horizons. He pointed out how many Negro postal clerks were being hired today.

I understand the youths' point of view. But I do sympathize with the senator.

Trouble was—he just didn't know to whom he was talking.

Someone should have given him a copy of the national magazine of J & J, which reads like a who's who in Negro society. You know—son of Mrs. so-and-so, Judge and Mrs. so-and-so, Attorney and Mrs. so-and-so, foreign exchange student so-and-so. Hardly a group that would aspire to be postal clerks. (Anyway, that's what we mothers like to think.)

Somebody should have told the senator that becoming a member of J & J is a little like being elected to Congress. Only worse. Your parents have to pass too. "What does her father do?" "Will his mother fit in?" And many there are who do not pass the test. Even the guest lists are carefully screened. I remember one occasion (and I like to think this was an individual reaction—not the consensus) when a girl was told not to invite her friend simply because the friend was white.

Suddenly I have become one of the "little" people. Me—the same gal who smirked superciliously when a Caucasian friend pointed out the discriminations in her own group—indicating that a cashmere sweater or a certain label in a tennis shoe were often the tickets to the "inner circle."

Now I reflect upon my own pettiness and wonder how I got here, and is it really worth it?

True, Elsie and Billy went to the J & J teenage conference last year with the group, got a look at Boulder Dam and Disneyland. And the twins attended the Portland Conference and spent a day at the Seattle World's Fair. I am sure they absorbed much culture—in fact they were bubbling over.

"You should have seen this Terry guy! He is *tough!*"

"Which workshop did you attend?"

"Huh? Oh, the one for the younger teenagers. We shoulda gone to that world affairs thing. Do you know Terry had a real mustache and he's only fourteen?"

"Did you enjoy the dinner dance?"

"Oh, yeah, and I didn't get to sew the straps on like you told me."

"You mean you wore it *strapless?*"

"Oh, gee, Mom, it was okay. You shoulda seen this cute guy. He was tough."

At this point Dad intervenes.

"How was the fair?"

"Tough. I rode on this one ride eight times. You see, it went down. . ."

"What did you see?"

"See? Oh, we walked around and looked at the exhibits."

"What country impressed you most?"

"Huh? Oh, I don't know which buildings we went in. But listen, we got in those little cars you drive yourself and . . ."

"You see," says my husband, "I told you you were wasting money."

Whereupon I point out that after all they are only thirteen and what thirteen-year-old, except a genius maybe, would prefer exhibits to rides, and all right, from now on I won't organize my children into anything. Billy is more enthusiastic about his integrated baseball team that he joined, and Elsie's eyes light up when she talks about the integrated interpretative dance group that she joined, and I decide maybe it's the same interests rather than the same color that bring together people who stimulate and bring out the best in one another. And why can't I keep my big mouth shut and learn to be more like my mama, who never joined anything for the sake of the children and whose only criteria for our friends was that they behave themselves? And anyway, who's to say who brings out the best in whom?

Elsie always studies better with the white girl up the street. And there was Susie.

Sweet, quiet, talented Susie, who would never have become best friends with Ginger except they were both colored and both in the same classroom. Their backgrounds were vastly different.

One night as I brushed Ginger's hair, I listened to her end of a telephone conversation with Susie.

"Do you have your report on the magazine article that's due tomorrow?"

"You don't? Well, look in *Life* or *Time*—they always have good articles."

"Oh, well, look in the *Reader's Digest*."

"You don't? Well, what do you have? Is that all?"

At this Ginger seemed at a loss, so I suggested the newspaper.

"Oh, Susie," she cried with relief, "look in the newspaper." Then incredulously, "You don't take a *newspaper?*"

Then she said with determination and understanding, "Never mind, I'll bring some magazines to school tomorrow and you can choose one."

And later at Christmastime, "Mama, I am going to give Susie a magazine subscription for Christmas."

Who grew more from this acquaintance—Ginger or Susie? I am not sure it is important. I just wish I knew when to direct and when to keep hands off.

Let them do their own joining. *I'll* concentrate on the basics—"brush your teeth, eat your dinner, tell the truth, get your lessons."

Top, Elsie and Billy; *bottom*, Patty-Jo and Ginger, 1962

9
No Wider Than the Heart Is Wide

Another trouble with being a mama is that life is so limited. The United Nations opens with East and West set to maneuver for the affections of millions of newly freed Africans; China is in the headlines; uncertainty looms in India; Democrats and Republicans wrangle in Congress; and all of it seems inconsequential in view of the earthshaking facts that Billy's knees have worn through his last pair of jeans, Ginger sat on the rented clarinet, and Elsie needs a new formal.

And somehow, somewhere, you remember hearing about *Dr. Zhivago* or *The Fire Next Time,* but who can read after struggling all evening with fractions or algebra? And it's not that you don't care about the president's program—it's just that you're having one heck of a time straightening out your own. And you certainly can't condemn any statesman for failure—you're too busy condemning yourself.

I'm convinced that my biggest trouble with being a mama is myself. Looking back, I am appalled at the things I didn't do. Looking ahead, I am scared of the things about which I don't know what to do.

I look over my teenage products.

I am proud of Elsie—her poise, her grace, her genuine understanding and deep compassion, her ability to put her finger on the core of why this person is that way. But I don't know what to do about her lack of confidence in herself, her difficulty in passing a test, any test, or her basic insecurity.

I am proud of Billy—his tall, handsome physique, his neat and clean-cut appearance (when he's properly dressed, I hasten to add), his sweetness and thoughtfulness that occasionally shine through in spite of himself, his quick mind, his loyalty to his friends, his concern about his sisters (though they'd never believe it), his sportsmanship. But I don't know what to do about his utter lack of responsibility, his "the world owes me a living" attitude, his terrible temper, or his indiscriminate choice of friends.

I am proud of Pat—her bubbling laughter and constant delight with life, her sharp artistic eye, her taste, her deftness and ability to do anything quickly and excellently, be it make a dress, draw a picture, write a paper, clean the kitchen cabinets, or set my hair. But I don't know what to do about her loudness, her concern about money and the things money can buy (tough car, tough shoes, neat skirt), her thinking only from the top of her mind.

I am proud of Ginger—her depth, her curiosity, her probing and ability to see beyond the surface in any personal, human, or social situation; her love of books and poetry; her wide vocabulary; her clever writing; her casual unconcern about things. But I don't know what to do about her loudness, her sloppiness, her tendency to bury herself in a book or a dream when the dishes need washing (or even when she's washing the dishes, and I guess that's why you have to wash everything you use after Ginger's dish day).

Now looking at all those talents and wonderful capabilities you'd think a really clever mother would be able to channel and direct, wouldn't you? Well, I guess a clever mother would. The trouble is I'm not really clever.

As a matter of fact, I'm not really anything.

Let's take a typical morning at my house.

No. Let's go from the sublime to the ridiculous. Let's take a typical morning at the house of one of the TV families.

I ask you, have you ever seen one of those darling mothers in curlers? You bet you haven't! There she stands all crisp and cool and calm and efficient, not even an eyelash out of place, table prettily set and ready for her slow but sure family who finally appear and, after a slightly funny family problem discussion, go their various ways with a wholesome, balanced breakfast under their belts.

Now take a typical morning at *my* house. Oh, I'm up early enough—the alarm rings at five and I arise and stagger across the house to Billy's room. And his room is *way* over on the other side of the house because when we built the house we copied somebody else's design, converting their workshop into a fourth bedroom, and wasn't that stupid when I need Billy where I can get my hands on him? Billy bumps his head on the bed and pleads for fifteen minutes more, and I wonder why in the world I ever thought an early morning paper route would develop responsibility. After about six shuttlings from my room to his, I decide if he's ever going to get to school on time, I'd better *drive* him on his paper route, so I do, waking up the girls on the way out. When we return, the twins' room and bath look like a shambles and they are busy combing their hair—you just can't possibly imagine, unless you have one of course, how long it takes a teenager to comb her hair! Elsie isn't up, so I get her up and start breakfast—two pieces of bacon, eggs, a pot of oatmeal, and two tuna sandwiches. (The bacon because *maybe* Elsie will eat eggs and bacon if she has time, oatmeal because hot cereal or waffles are all Billy will eat and we don't have time for the latter, tuna sandwiches because the twins have to catch the bus at 7:45, and if lucky they will have just finished their hair by then, and they can take the sandwiches with them.) Nothing for Bill because he's out of town as usual. Meanwhile Billy wants a shirt ironed, and while I'm doing that the twins leave without their sandwiches. Billy starts his shower, and Elsie combs her hair in my bathroom. By the time Billy has dawdled through his shower, his dressing, and breakfast (being the only one with a balanced breakfast if one can call three bowls of oatmeal balanced), I have decided if he is ever going to make German at all, I'll have to drive him. Elsie grabs one of the tuna sandwiches and is off with us. After dropping them at two different schools, I return exhausted to a ringing phone, which is Pat who forgot her algebra book and must have it immediately and would I please?

And all the while keeps running through my mind the refrain—too late, too late. Too late to produce perfect children. I'd have to be perfect myself. And, in a rare moment of truth, I face the fact that I am not, never was, and never will be. And, in my most depressing moments, I think perhaps I should have taken a job and let somebody else rear my children. But I didn't. And there they are. All imperfect like me. And all almost ready to face the world on their own.

And then I begin to take a look at that world out there.

That's another thing about being a mama. You learn how in stages—one stage behind. You don't think about the world. Just eat a good dinner, scrub your elbows, get your lessons.

Then something happens. Suddenly one day your loved ones begin to venture out, and you realize that your life extends beyond the ironing board. Suddenly come brief illuminating flashes of the cord that stretches from you to there.

Especially if you are colored.

How could you be oblivious to all that is going on in the world today if you are colored?

The headlines race across the pages:

"Dixie Race Incident Erupts with Bomb"

"Birmingham Cops Use Hose on Demonstrating Negroes"

"Carolina White Slain in Racial Riot"

"Alabama Governor Moves to Block Integration at University of Alabama"

"Police Quell Negro Voter Registration Demonstrations at Greensboro"

"Demonstrating Negroes Are Jailed by the Thousands"

"CORE Students in California Capitol Sit-In to Urge Passage of Anti-Discrimination Housing Bill"

"Tallahassee Negroes Parade Before Segregated Theaters"

"Negro NAACP Leader Slain in Jackson, Mississippi"

"Black Muslim's Cry Grows Louder—'The White Devil's Day Is Almost Over'"

These years of protest and violence make us remember Adolf Hitler's liquidation of the Warsaw Jewish ghetto. An editorial in a local paper observes: "Nor must the world ever forget the attempted liquidation of a whole race of people. It is not enough to say that it cannot happen again. The lesson of history is that it could, for it happened once."

It was the Nazis who trained dogs to attack at the word "Jew." It was Birmingham policemen who set snarling dogs on Negroes demonstrating for equal rights.

Some of the pictures speak louder than words—the one of a lone Negro woman, a would-be voter, being manhandled by white policemen; the one of water hoses tearing off the clothes of Negro demonstrators; the one of an unresisting Negro being kicked in the face by a white man while others stand by laughing.

All of us are concerned. The integrationists who have pledged themselves not to turn back, the segregationists who as yet have achieved no standard (as I once heard a lecturer say) to release them from being *only* white, the southern governors with their "sovereign" states, the president with his national policy. All of us wonder what will happen next.

The truth is that many different things will happen. Contrary to one man's opinion, we are *not* a nation of sheep. And we will fight our battles as individuals according to what we are.

It takes a certain type of man, one already full of hurt and hate and personal vengeance, to tear a Jewish baby in half, to lynch an Emmett Till. Just as it takes a certain type of man to passively resist, like the Negro students who trained themselves not to strike back and the white college professor who joined the sit-ins in Jackson, Mississippi, and did not resist even when his face was beaten raw and salt poured in his wounds.

So we will choose up sides and be what we already are.

Some of us, with hearts so full of hurt and hate and bigotry and violence that it all must explode somewhere, will join the Black Muslims or the Ku Klux Klan.

Some of us will preach hate and racial supremacy, like Ross Barnett and Malcolm X.

Some of us will preach love and respect for ourselves and others, like Pope John XXIII and Martin Luther King.

Some of us will be victims caught in the maelstrom of bitter, blind prejudice, like Emmett Till, the black boy who was lynched in Mississippi, and Paul Guihard, the French newspaperman killed on the Mississippi campus.

Some of us will be martyrs in a dedicated, to-the-death fight for human dignity, like William Moore, the crusading white postman murdered near Attalla, Alabama, and Medgar Evers, the Negro NAACP field secretary who was murdered in Jackson, Mississippi.

Some of us, like Ralph McGill and James Baldwin, will sway men toward right and reason with eloquent words.

Some of us, black and white, will march, sit in, demonstrate, and go to jail for what we believe is right and to make our democracy a living reality.

But most of us, black and white, will be just plain people—teachers and students, doctors, laborers, lawyers, insurance salesmen, and mamas and papas—more interested in the mortgage payment and whether Tommy's teeth need straightening than in what Governor Wallace said on television last night. And what we plain ordinary people feel in our hearts will count more than all the efforts of all the extremists put together. Remember:

And, as a single leaf turns not yellow
but with the silent knowledge of the whole tree,
So the wrong-doer cannot do wrong
without the hidden will of you all.

It took a certain type of man to commit the mass murder of innocent men, women, and children in Nazi Germany; but thousands of just plain people had to close their eyes to the throngs riding past their doors to the gas chambers, and thousands of just plain people had to ignore the stench from the human pyres.

The night that I watched Vivian Malone walk like a model into the University of Alabama, past Governor Wallace and the mob and the troops that surrounded her, tears came into my eyes—tears of pride and fear. I cannot help but believe that somewhere, perhaps in the South, a white mother, simply because she was a mother, also watched with tears of pride and fear.

Once I attended a writing class where we read and criticized each other's stories. One night I read one of my stories called "Madge and the Lemon Cream Pie," a rather charming story (I thought) carrying a subtle message about prejudice. After class, a lady refugee from an oppressed land came up to me—intense and angry.

"You should not write about prejudice and lemon cream pies. The message is too *big*, too *important* for that. Do not confuse it with *small* things."

But I cannot help it. I believe prejudice or nonprejudice is inevitably entwined in the small area of everyday living—the church, the school, the PTA, the boy next door, the girl in my class, the man across the street, the man I work for, the man who works for me, the girl who came home with the children, the group in the picnic area next to me. Here at home and in the streets and the marketplaces the real battle for human dignity is being fought. It's not always easy to be on the right side. Especially for a mama.

It takes mamas a long time to grow up. We tend to cling to the good as we know it, the best as we see it, the familiar, the happy. We try to weave a protective cocoon of what we think is safe and happy to guard our children from the world out there.

I too am guilty. My children finally make me realize this is not what they want or indeed what they need. It is they who finally say, "For goodness sake, let the world come in."

Oh, not in those exact words. In phrases such as "You're prejudiced, Mama. Always talking about how great the Negro is. They're just like other people" and "You're so *snooty*, Mama. Always wanting to know who somebody's mama is."

And as my children teach me, they free me. I leave the segregated Negro church located on the other side of town and join the church only a block away from my home, not because it is predominantly white but because it is of the same faith and I can get there on time. Besides, with three daughters and weddings in mind, there is nothing like belonging to a church only one block away. I no longer affiliate with groups or individuals because they are colored and "I like my own kind" or because they're predominantly white and "I should integrate" but because the group is worthwhile or I like the individual. I have resigned from the select Negro group formed for the cultural and social benefit of my children mainly because my children seldom attended the meetings. I welcome all the teenagers, black and white, who flock to my home despite my husband's admonitions to "please inform them this is not the YMCA day room." Among my Mother's Day gifts was a box of candy with a card that read, "To our second mother" from "your other sons." I was especially proud that it was signed by two of my favorites, one black boy and one white boy, neither of whose parents I know. It was like receiving a diploma.

And the children, what have they learned from me?

I would like to tell you, especially as a Negro mother, that they are wonderful, ambitious, talented children who will accomplish great and wonderful things, who will always deserve the rights and privileges afforded to all the citizens of our great democracy. But I can only tell you that they are human as are your own children, with the same potentials, the same frailties. I look at them—all imperfect, all about to face an imperfect world. I labor hard to overcome their imperfections. Until one day, with deep humility, I realize that I don't know an imperfection from an asset.

For once in a great while I get a bright promise of what my children may become. And more often than not it is what I consider a fault that makes the promise.

Like Ginger and her daydreaming.

"Deidre and I were talking," she says one day.

"Deidre and Ginger are always talking," says my surface-minded Pat, "about a lot of dumb stuff—Russia and Cubans and races and junk."

"About the Cubans and communism," continues Ginger, unperturbed. "We wrote a letter to the newspaper. Would you like to hear it?"

I would.

It reads: "Dear Sir: We believe the biggest problem facing the world today is man's prejudice, which is usually against something he knows nothing about. Sometimes, after persecution and unwarranted oppression, people are willing to trade political freedom for equal opportunities and full stomachs. The Cubans may have a dictator now, but they also have what they believe is equality and education, which are things they did not have before. We believe America's biggest threat to communism lies in its treatment of minority groups."

I suppose the fact that Deidre is Chinese and Ginger is Negro is somehow significant, but for the moment I think only of Ginger—daydreaming big things about Cubans and

Russians, empty stomachs, and national policy. She may never get the dishes clean, but her thoughts will soar, across the land and the nation, above classes and creeds and color of skin. And Billy.

"I like Marshall," says Pat of one of Billy's white friends, "he's not at all prejudiced!"

"Whaddaya mean, he's not prejudiced!" exclaims Billy. "He just doesn't *think* about it."

I listen to Billy pay his friend the supreme compliment and realize that it is a compliment he could pay himself. How I have lamented his indiscriminate choice of friends! The fact is, he just doesn't think about it—how rich, how poor, how smart, how lazy, how black, how white. And maybe this is more good than bad.

I don't know if Billy will ever be famous or rich. Right now, frankly, I'm worried about his getting out of high school. But I know that he has a heart unblemished by crippling prejudices.

And I think that if I could choose the one quality I would like my son to have in this crazy, mixed-up world, that would be it—a heart unblemished by crippling prejudices. It not only assures me that he'll never be a Hitler or a Malcolm X but also that he is free—the whole wide world of all mankind is open to him.

Seated, Bill and Eva; *standing* Ginger, Billy, Patty-Jo, and Elsie,

Sacramento, Easter 1958

10
We, the People

Those young people of today and of a few years back—you read about them in your newspapers. Maybe you read about them as I did, with memories flooding your heart.

I remember the walk to the segregated school. One high school, comparatively new, for all the Negroes of crowded Atlanta—no gym, no auditorium, no cafeteria. Even now I can remember the crowding, pushing, human flesh that squeezed through the halls during class changes. I remember pushing down the crowded steps, out the back door, gathering around an improvised counter in the back of the school to get lunch that had been prepared in the little ten by twelve kitchen—doughnuts, milk, hamburgers, soup. You ate standing up—sometimes in the drizzling rain.

I remember being hot and tired and hungry in the middle of a shopping spree—no place to eat, no place to rest.

I remember passing the lovely public park on a hot humid day, gazing longingly at the white children cavorting in the pool.

I remember the push to the back of the bus. I remember standing in a railroad station tired and sick—holding for support to the hand of my little girl—as the clerk told me no pullman reservations were available for Thursday.

"When?" I asked.

"Not for three months," he answered.

I stared at the clerk, listened to him tell that lie, knew it was a lie, and felt helpless against it. It was not anger I felt— only fear. Please, my heart cried, I have to go and I'm scared and sick, and I can't go that far in a crowded "jim crow" car. But my heart cried in silence, and the clerk turned away.

I should have known better. I knew that Negroes could only receive first-class treatment through subterfuge. You called on the phone for reservations and sent a "boy" to pick up the tickets, or if you were fair enough you "passed." My own cousins often did. And I recall the tale of a former coworker about a train ride when she was five.

Her mother cautioned her before a train trip, "Now, Mary Elizabeth, we are going to pretend you're *white*. Don't say *anything* about being colored."

They boarded the train, and all went well until Mary Elizabeth asked for and was refused a piece of candy. Angry and anxious to get even with her mother, she began to chant, softly at first, then louder, "I ain't nuthin' buta old black nigger, I ain't nuthin' buta old black . . ." Whereupon her mother clapped her hand over her mouth, retreated with her to the ladies' room, and proceeded to paddle until Mary Elizabeth conceded, "Okay, Mama, I'm white folks."

But I was only a "black nigger" and could be mistaken for nothing else. So I stood, silent and scared.

"Do you want to phone for reservations?" asked my father. "I'll go down and pick them up."

But I was too weak to fight, even with subterfuge. What would happen if they put me off the train?

My dear kind father understood. "We'll get plane tickets," he said. "I'll pay the extra."

So one bright morning with my knees knocking and holding tight to my baby's hand I boarded a plane for the first time in my life. It was a surprisingly delightful trip. However, we had to stop over in the Cincinnati airport, and from there our reservations had not been confirmed. We went into the airport dining room for dinner. All eyes focused upon us. I thought we looked rather chic in our mother and daughter suits of black and white checks, and I hoped the glances were of admiration but in my nervous state could not be sure. I do know I was aware of considerable consternation and delay before we were served and that the waitress was especially haughty and rude. I bent over backwards to be gracious and grateful and requested my daughter to "thank the kind lady for serving you so nicely." As I tipped her before we left, the waitress said, "I think you and I could get along"—whatever that meant.

So it was with memories flooding my heart that I turned away from my favorite store—the five-and-ten. I knew what these young people were fighting for.

Still I pretended that the problem was far, far away.

Even earlier, faced with the controversy over the integrated school, I thanked God that we were not involved. I shielded the children from the headlines.

Elsie was a big girl then—grown tall and slender and graceful—with a smooth, tan complexion and quiet, eager brown eyes, with warmth and a certain sensitivity that made her particularly vulnerable to the world about her. She was thirteen, poised in that brief flight from childhood to adulthood, an age where little things counted more—and the opinions of one's contemporaries most of all; where one's dress, shoes, and hair style must fit the pattern; where it was a crime to be different, apart, and a world without a pal was no world at all.

And there was Billy with his energy, his happy smile, his utter absorption with Little League, and his pals, black and white, who ran in and out of the house.

And the twins—roly-poly young Brownies. "We're the only real Brownies in the troop," they would say, "brown all over."

So I, in my selfishness, thanked God that the children were in California, away from the controversy, the ugly strife and turmoil that surrounded boys and girls in some parts of our nation.

But as I read the papers, I could not be impartial. I read with horror of the bombings, the rioting, the troops called out, what the president said or didn't say, the comments of the attorney general, this judge, that governor.

But the children—they interested me most. I thought of the white children forced into a situation foreign to their nature, a bitterness and prejudice unnatural to the freshness and innocence of youth. I studied the picture of a pretty young white girl as she stood calmly, courageously, before a group of the White Citizens Council and said, "I don't think segregation is Christian." I read of other white teenagers who were speaking out publicly for integration in spite of the violent forces that opposed it. I looked at the pictures of the black boys and girls walking alone to classes, proceeding courageously through a sea of hatred and bitterness, and I thought, there but for the grace of God go mine.

In my heart, I walked with them—the Bobby Cains, the Dorothy Counts, all of them. But, in my heart, I was glad that mine were not among them—so sensitive, so vulnerable, so easily hurt. Would I have the courage to send them? I wondered. Would they have the courage to go?

I thought of the little boy faced with bayonets on the opening day of school. "Are you afraid?" asked his father.

"Yes," answered the boy, "I'm scared of Latin!"

I turned back to the pictures and studied them closely—these boys and girls like mine, just as sensitive, just as vulnerable. But they did not seem afraid! An inner strength seemed to emanate from their faces and a gentle, quiet calmness placed them apart. Why, I wondered, why weren't they afraid?

It was Elsie who supplied the answer—with no idea that she did so—casually, lightly, one day as we were eating dinner.

"Oh, Mama," she said, "our social studies are real interesting now. We're studying the Constitution."

"Yes?" I answered, as I dished up rice and admonished Billy to please eat with a fork.

"Yeah, Mama, do you know why they made a Constitution?"

"Well . . ." Did I?

"You see they thought with so many little states, they wouldn't have a chance if somebody attacked them. So they joined together to be stronger and wrote the Constitution. We've got to learn it by heart."

"The whole Constitution?"

"And a lot of men signed it—Thomas Jefferson and . . ."

"And Abraham Lincoln," supplied Ginger.

"Don't be silly," said Elsie. "He wasn't even born then."

And then it came to me—that was it—the force behind the calm, resolute faces. Those boys and girls in Tennessee, North Carolina, and Arkansas were reading the same history books that Elsie was reading, and that history was embedded in their hearts and minds—the Declaration of Independence, the Constitution of the United States, the Bill of Rights. I borrowed Elsie's book.

"We hold these truths to be self evident, that all men are created equal, that they are endowed by their Creator with certain unalienable Rights."

They had heard the words of our great ones. Down through the ages has come the voice of Patrick Henry: "Is life so dear or peace so sweet as to be purchased at the price of chains and slavery? Forbid it, Almighty God! I know not what course others may take; but as for me, give me liberty or give me death!"

They read of a civil war that tore our country apart, a war to free the slaves and to preserve the Union, that "government of the people, by the people, and for the people, shall not perish from the earth."

Even Ginger, in the fourth grade, knew about Abraham Lincoln: "It is for us the living, rather, to be dedicated here to the unfinished work which they who fought here, have thus far so nobly advanced."

For us the living. The children read the books, hear the words, and believe them. We, the adults, appear to have forgotten. Has the roar of the politician fanning the fire of racism, the age-old herring dragged through election campaigns from Chickamauga to Little Rock, from Los Angeles to New York City—to which the hoodlum element and reactionaries fall easy prey—deluded thinking Americans too? Or are we, in our comfortable homes, more concerned with the mere exigencies of living—the mortgage, car payment, taxes, floor polish, did I call the cleaners? Perhaps we're too far removed from the foundation of our government and what is going on about us.

But the children—the children are learning the Constitution. They believe that we shall live up to the laws we have made. They believe in this nation, this lighthouse across the sea, saying to the oppressed of Hungary and Syria, "Give me your tired, your poor, your huddled masses yearning to breathe free." The children have faith.

And the children have learned their history well. They are not afraid of bigots and hoodlums. In this land of the free and home of the brave, in this land of equal opportunity, the white children are not afraid to speak for what they believe to be right, and the black children are mainly concerned with how they will measure up. Will they pass the test—reading, writing, and Latin?

They walk proudly, these children of freedom; calmly, confidently, through the rabble-rousers, their faces toward the sun, courageously, quietly, as if they could see a flag waving and hear a band playing. And we have followed where they led.

I passed the five-and-ten, and on vacation in Atlanta, I passed it again, as I did all the downtown stores.

"We don't stop there," said my friends, "not until we can eat there."

And they would smile.

"No one eats there."

'Why?"

"Because whenever they open the counters the students move in and sit."

The sit-ins, remember them?

"There is not an eating place open in downtown Atlanta."

My heart thrilled. I knew for what they fought.

"Where can I buy a pair of stockings?"

They led me far on the outskirts of town.

Last week a friend of mine returned from a visit to Atlanta.

"I had dinner at the top of the . . . (in the middle of down-town Atlanta) and lunch at . . . (he mentioned one of the biggest downtown stores in Atlanta)."

And five young Negroes have been admitted to Georgia Tech, and one is at Emory's Medical School.

My heart almost burst with pride.

The kids had done it. These young courageous Negroes of today—quietly, nonviolently. With dignity they had attained a dignity heretofore reserved for "white folks."

But was it only the kids? Could we forget the long strug-gle of the NAACP climaxing with the Supreme Court deci-sion of 1954, the decision that opened the doors for these brave children?

And other adults, like Rosa Parks, set an example. Rosa Parks, the seamstress in Montgomery, Alabama, who was tired one day and refused to relinquish her seat on the bus. Was she physically tired? Had her sewing that day been espe-cially tedious? Did she just want to close her eyes and relax for those brief moments while the bus sped her to her destina-tion? Or was she weary with a great soul-searching weariness? Weary of standing while others sat? Weary of being pushed to the back of the bus? Weary of relinquishing her dignity for the vanity of others?

She perhaps had no idea as she sat that day on the bus that she would start a new movement, a new philosophy of nonviolent direct action, a movement that was to sweep across the country capturing many people in its wake, a movement headed by Martin Luther King, the Gandhi of the Negro people of the United States.

Like a fever that must run its course before it burns itself out—or like a fever that will not burn itself out—this new movement swept across the country.

And we Negroes who were not on the firing lines watched with the rest of the world, watched and gloated with pride—the sit-ins, the freedom riders—as Negro citizens all over the South for the first time *demanded* equal treatment.

By the time the demonstrators reached Birmingham we were a little weary of it all.

"Why don't the segregationists *give* up?"

"Why don't the Negroes *let* up?"

Even I, even I.

"What are they demonstrating for *now?*" I asked my husband as King and his followers moved into Birmingham.

He looked at me strangely.

"Everything," he said quietly.

So I did not admit what I was really thinking—if only it were a *particular* store or a lunch counter or something *specific—this* mass demonstration seemed so pointless, so general, so disorganized.

Though Bull Connor with his dogs and his water hose inflamed me and roused my sympathy for my people, still the quiet voice within me asked, *was this trip necessary?* What was the *point?*

And there was this other thing. Perhaps because I was born there, spent some of the happiest years of my life there, because my mother and father lie buried there—I really don't *know* why—but I love the South. Somehow, in any discussion I seem to rise to its defense.

"These are not all of the people," I said of Bull Connor and his rabid segregationists. I clung to one small picture printed during a lull in the Birmingham battle. It was a picture of a policeman watching casually and friendly while two little Negro boys played baseball nearby. Something about it brought back a peaceful happy childhood lived in the South.

Could I have forgotten so soon?

A line from what we used to call the "Negro national anthem" comes to me. We don't sing this anthem very much now because it is not seemly for citizens of the United States to have a special national anthem. But in my southern, segregated school days we sang it often, and it is one of the most beautiful songs ever written. There are two lines that go,

> Lest our feet stray from the places, our God,
>   where we met Thee,
> Lest, our hearts drunk with the wine of the world,
>   we forget Thee.

Had I strayed so far?

Had I forgotten so soon?

Two things made me remember.

One small picture appeared in a writer's magazine. The magazine had offered a prize for the best caption. It was a picture of several Negro youths, young boys and girls about the age of Elsie, leaning against a building while the fierce water from a fire hose beat upon their bodies and ripped their clothes. The winning caption read, "We, the people of the United States."

How could I have thought that there had to be something *specific* to demonstrate about?

We, the people of the United States. We have certain inalienable rights, guaranteed by the Constitution of the United States—to vote, to live where we choose, to study where we choose, to work, to play, to love, to marry whom we please. And we the people of the United States will *not* let up until we enjoy these rights.

How could I have forgotten so soon?

The other thing that made me remember came on a Sunday morning.

Bill and I were riding across the Yolo causeway. He often accuses me of being too much a mama and arranges expeditions that will take me away from the children.

"This Sunday," he said, "you and I will have dinner in San Francisco."

It was a lovely sunny day in California. We were enjoying the drive—not even knowing where we would eat and scarcely conscious of the special privilege we enjoyed of being able to eat anywhere. We were enjoying the scenery, casually chatting, listening to the radio.

At first I wasn't sure I heard right, or maybe I didn't want to believe it.

"Sixteenth Street Baptist Church bombed in Birmingham. Four girls killed. Negro youth shot by policeman. Another Negro youth on bicycle killed."

Like quicksilver the shock of it tore through my body. All I could think was, those poor, poor young children; those mothers! And next came the stabbing thought, *it could have been my girls*—Pat and Ginger, fourteen. The boy could have been Billy.

There but for the grace of God.

Bill and I had both lived and worked in Birmingham, many times had attended the Sixteenth Street Baptist Church, would perhaps still be there if Bill had gotten the job he had applied for, right outside of Birmingham. At the time we were disappointed.

For it is not true that Negroes stay in the South or run away from the South. Like everyone else, we move where destiny takes us. The crop is bad and we move away from the country. No job to be had and we move farther north. The Air Force moves and we move with it. And we are here instead of there.

And for the very first time on that Sunday morning of September 15, 1963, I admitted that I was glad.

For on this Sunday morning I came face to face with my beloved South. It is not calm and peaceful. It is like a sleeping volcano that erupts suddenly and violently when you least expect it. A volcano that destroys whatever is in its way.

And it has always been thus. How could I have forgotten?

The fear that was ever there, though you couldn't touch it or even explain it, as though you were always on a tightrope and must never sway too far this way or that. If you rode the bus, you sat in the back. You didn't *try* to eat at a lunch counter. You didn't go where you were not wanted. You avoided trouble as much as you could.

And the fear was ever present because no matter who you were or where you lived, deep in your heart you knew trouble could strike anywhere. Because you were who you were.

One day, when I was a very little girl, trouble was the brutal murder of the brother of one of my good friends, son of a school principal. He was playing in a park across the street from his home, unaware that another Negro boy had been there before him and had made derogatory remarks to two white couples as they walked out of the woods beyond. One white man had gone to get his gun, returned, and shot the wrong boy. For weeks the threat of a race riot hung over Atlanta. My father brought a gun home for the first time.

And one bright sunny day when I was about fourteen, a white girl and I sat at my kitchen table munching apples. She had come over to use the phone as she and her sisters often did. They had many boyfriends who were always calling on our phone. This day we looked up to see a burly white policeman climbing in the kitchen window brandishing a gun. Another came down the front hall. They had received a call that "white girls were meeting colored men" at our house. They took her home, ignoring my mother and me completely. Next day the girls were back, saying that it was their girlfriend's mother down the street who had phoned the police and not to pay her any mind, she was just jealous of their popularity. But Mama would never let them come over again. She was keenly aware of what we had escaped simply because our menfolk were not at home. One of my handsome brothers had just dressed and gone whistling down the street to his girlfriend's house a narrow few minutes before the policemen arrived.

You are ever aware that however respectable you might be, in the eyes of some you are still a *big black nigger*, better expressed in the words of a policeman who stopped my husband and some of his college classmates in Atlanta. The driver of the car, in response to the policeman's "What's your name, nigger?" replied, "William Augustus Bell the second." Whereupon the policeman yelled, "Willy, nigger, Willy! Ain't no niggers called William!" Incidentally, "Willy" was the son of a college president.

And on that September Sunday, I admitted that I was not brave enough nor good enough. I could not love my enemies. If it were Pat or Billy or any of mine, I would scream and fight and *kill!* I could not peacefully resist.

But my heart salutes those who can.

Others salute them too. Like Eddie Dickerson, the white boy who fought against the freedom riders and was so impressed by the fact that they did not strike back that he joined CORE (Congress of Racial Equality) to help the cause of racial equality. While demonstrating with them in Cambridge, Maryland, against a restaurant, he was slapped in the face with a raw egg by the proprietor. Now, reports a magazine, it is the proprietor who regrets it. "I am so ashamed," he said afterward, "makes me feel less than a man."

So the demonstrations serve not only the Negroes but white citizens as well. They make the government of the people for the people come true.

A few days ago my husband brought three visiting conferees home for dinner—all white. I went on an errand and returned to find all of them on the patio at the Ping-Pong table—all but one, a young captain. In the family room, alone, he was eagerly reading my *Crisis*, the NAACP magazine.

He looked at me rather shamefacedly. "I don't dare read this at home," he said. "I'm from Alabama. I'm so proud of King. I have a friend—a Negro—used to be a waiter at a club. Now he's a lawyer fighting for civil rights. I sneak out to see him when I am home."

And my Texan neighbor, also white, reveals that her husband's company might transfer him to Texas.

"How nice," say I, "you'll be home near your mother."

"Oh, I don't want to go to Texas," she said.

"Why?" I asked.

"Well, I don't see us taking this ride in Texas," she said. With our husbands, we were taking a very pleasant ride down the river to a local steakhouse.

It occurred to me then that several white people were also yearning to be free, to read what they like, believe what they like, see whom they like.

When I watched on television the march on Washington, I was proud. I was proud of all the speakers, of Marian Anderson, whose beautiful voice rang out in song. I was proud of the rabbi who reminded us of what happened in Germany. I was proud of Martin Luther King as he said, "Let freedom ring!"

But most of all I was proud of the people, black and white, who stood in the sweltering sun, tired and weary, quiet and dignified, saying more eloquently than words ever could, *We, the people of the United States.*

About the Author

EVA RUTLAND was born in Atlanta, Georgia, in a house built by her grandfather, a former slave. Her father, Samuel Neal, was a pharmacist, and her mother, Eva Westmoreland Neal, a teacher.

She attended a private elementary school and Washington High, the only public high school for Atlanta's Negroes at the time. In 1937, she received a bachelor's degree from Spelman College, with a major in economics and a minor in English and drama.

Eva Rutland has been telling stories all of her life. Her first published piece was "A Christmas Story," which appeared in the *Atlanta Daily World*, Atlanta's black newspaper, when she was about twelve. She began to write seriously when her children were young, in an attempt to promote more understanding between black and white mothers. The first of these articles, "Elsie and God," appeared in *Redbook* magazine in 1952. Her first book, *The Trouble with Being a Mama*, was published in 1964.

She sold her first romance in 1985 and has published more than twenty books since. Her *Choices* was one of the three novellas in *Girl Friends,* which was a finalist for outstanding fiction in the NAACP Image Awards, 1999. She received the 2000 Golden Pen Award for Lifetime Achievement. She married William Rutland in 1943. She lives in Sacramento, California, and has four adult children, six grandchildren, and one great-granddaughter.